Concepts
for Today

Third Edition

Reading for Today SERIES, BOOK 4

LORRAINE C. SMITH

AND

NANCY NICI MARE

English Language Institute
Queens College
The City University of New York

HEINLE
CENGAGE Learning

Australia • Brazil • Japan • Korea • Mexico • Singapore • Spain • United Kingdom • United States

HEINLE
CENGAGE Learning™

Reading for Today 4: Concepts for Today
Third Edition
Lorraine C. Smith and Nancy Nici Mare

Publisher, the Americas, Global, and Dictionaries: Sherrise Roehr

Acquisitions Editor: Thomas Jefferies

Senior Development Editor:
Laura Le Dréan

Senior Content Project Manager:
Maryellen E. Killeen

Director of U.S. Marketing:
James McDonough

Senior Product Marketing Manager:
Katie Kelley

Academic Marketing Manager:
Caitlin Driscoll

Director of Global Marketing: Ian Martin

Senior Print Buyer: Betsy Donaghey

Compositor: Pre-PressPMG

Cover and Interior Design: Muse Group

Library of Congress Control Number: 2010925343

ISBN–13: 978-1-111-03305-7

ISBN–10: 1-111-03305-6

Heinle
20 Channel Center Street
Boston, MA 02210
USA

Cengage Learning is a leading provider of customized learning solutions with office locations around the globe, including Singapore, the United Kingdom, Australia, Mexico, Brazil, and Japan. Locate your local office at: **international.cengage.com/region**

Cengage Learning products are represented in Canada by Nelson Education, Ltd.

For your course and learning solutions, visit **academic.cengage.com**

Purchase any of our products at your local college store or at our preferred online store **www.CengageBrain.com**

Printed in Canada
1 2 3 4 5 6 7 8 9 14 13 12 11 10

CREDITS

Skills Chart   ix
Preface   xiii
Introduction   xvi
Acknowledgments   xxi

UNIT 1 Living in Society   1

Chapter 1 **The Paradox of Happiness**   2
by Diane Swanbrow, in *Psychology Today*
*New research reveals a surprising truth: the tendency
to feel unhappy may be inherited, but happiness is
something that we can create for ourselves.*

Chapter 2 **Junior Status: Sharing Dad's Name a Mixed Bag**   20
by Melissa Dahl, *MSNBC*
*Being given the same name as his father has its
up side and down side for José Martinez, Jr.
and many others.*

Chapter 3 **The Birth-Order Myth**   36
by Alfie Kohn, in *Health*
*Although many people think that being the
first, second, or third child in a family affects
our personalities, such beliefs are really untrue.*

UNIT 2 Health and Well-Being   57

Chapter 4 **Laughter Is the Best Medicine for Your Heart**   58
by Michelle W. Murray
*Exercising and eating healthy food can reduce the
risk of heart disease, but is laughter important,
too? Cardiologists have discovered that laughter
and an active sense of humor may also help
protect against a heart attack.*

Chapter 5   **Acupuncture: The New Old Medicine**   **74**
             Edited by William G. Flanagan, in *Forbes*
                Many people today are discovering that
                acupuncture can cure illnesses that
                conventional medical treatment cannot cure.
                It's also inexpensive and almost painless.

Chapter 6   **Highs and Lows in Self-Esteem**   **96**
             by Kim Lamb Gregory, Scripps Howard
             News Service
                During our lives, we experience periods of high
                self-esteem and low self-esteem because we
                are affected by biological, social, and
                situational factors.

UNIT 3   # Government and Education   117

Chapter 7   **The Federal System of Government**   **118**
             by Patricia C. Acheson, from Our Federal
             Government: How It Works
                The U.S. Government was designed over 200
                years ago. It has a complex, but effective,
                system of checks and balances to ensure that
                no one has too much power.

Chapter 8   **Teachers Are Key for Students**   **142**
             by Greg Toppo, in *USA Today*
                Why is school so difficult for many students?
                Some believe it is the teacher's challenge to
                engage all students in the learning process.

Chapter 9   **The Pursuit of Excellence**   **158**
             by Jill Smolowe, in *Time*
                Every year, thousands of foreign students come to
                the United States to study in American universities
                and colleges in search of an education.

UNIT 4   # Science and Technology   181

Chapter 10   **Antarctica: Whose Continent Is It Anyway?**   182
              by Daniel and Sally Grotta, in *Popular Science*
              *Although an international treaty helps protect
              the continent of Antarctica, countries still argue
              over who has the right to live and work there.*

Chapter 11   **A Messenger from the Past**   199
              by James Shreeve, in *Discover*
              *When the frozen body of a man was discovered
              in a melting glacier at the border between Austria
              and Italy, scientists began to learn about life in
              Europe over 5,000 years ago.*

Chapter 12   **Is Time Travel Possible?**   218
              by Mark Davidson, in *USA Today*
              *Some scientific experiments have shown that
              time travel may be possible. Scientists discuss
              the possible consequences of traveling to the
              past or to the future.*

Index of Key Words and Phrases   241
Skills Index   247

Unit	Chapter and Title	Reading Skills Focus	Structure Focus	Follow-up Activities Skills Focus
Unit 1 **Living in Society** *Page 1*	**Chapter 1** **The Paradox of Happiness** *Page 2*	• Preview reading to activate background knowledge • Analyze reading through True / False, Multiple Choice, and Short Answer questions • Use context clues to understand and use vocabulary • Use dictionary entries to select synonyms and accurate definitions • Identify main ideas and details • Organize information using an outline • Use outline notes to recall and summarize information	• Recognize and use the suffixes: *-ance, -ence, -ion,* and *-tion* • Identify and use parts of speech: nouns and verbs • Use singular and plural nouns • Use correct verb tenses	• *Critical Thinking:* Express opinions supported by examples; compare and contrast ideas • *Writing:* Write a summary, write an opinion composition with supporting examples; write a journal entry
	Chapter 2 **Junior Status: Sharing Dad's Name a Mixed Bag** *Page 20*	• Preview reading to activate background knowledge • Analyze reading through True / False, Multiple Choice, and Short Answer questions • Use context clues to understand and use vocabulary • Use dictionary entries to select synonyms and accurate definitions • Scan for main ideas and skim for details • Organize information into a chart • Use chart to recall and summarize information	• Recognize and use the suffixes: *-ion* and *-tion* • Identify and use parts of speech: nouns and verbs • Use singular and plural nouns • Use correct verb tenses	• *Critical Thinking:* Identify and understand inference; support answers with examples • *Writing:* Write a summary; write a journal entry; write an opinion composition with supporting examples
	Chapter 3 **The Birth-Order Myth** *Page 36*	• Preview reading to activate background knowledge • Analyze reading through True / False, Multiple Choice, and Short Answer questions • Use context clues to understand vocabulary and punctuation marks • Use dictionary entries to select synonyms and accurate definitions • Take notes from reading and organize information using an outline • Use an outline to recall and summarize information	• Recognize and use the noun suffixes: *-ment* and *-ce* • Identify and use parts of speech: nouns, verbs, and adjectives	• *Critical Thinking:* Identify and understand inference; express opinions supported with examples; draw conclusions • *Writing:* Write an opinion paragraph with examples; analyze and record results of a survey • *Discussion:* Compare opinions about advantages and disadvantages; discuss survey results

Unit	Chapter and Title	Reading Skills Focus	Structure Focus	Follow-up Activities Skills Focus
Unit 2 **Health and Well-Being** *Page 57*	**Chapter 4** **Laughter Is the Best Medicine for Your Heart** *Page 58*	• Preview reading to activate background knowledge • Analyze reading through True / False, Multiple Choice, and Short Answer questions • Use context clues to understand vocabulary • Use dictionary entries to select synonyms and accurate definitions • Scan for details • Organize information using a chart • Use notes from chart to recall and summarize information	• Recognize and use the suffix: *-ity* • Correctly identify and use parts of speech: nouns, verbs, and adjectives	• *Critical Thinking:* Identify and understand inferences; express opinions supported with examples; draw conclusions • *Writing:* Write a summary; write an opinion paragraph supported with examples; write a journal entry • *Discussion:* Describe a movie
	Chapter 5 **Acupuncture: The New Old Medicine** *Page 74*	• Use prereading questions to activate background knowledge • Analyze reading through True / False, Multiple Choice, and Short Answer questions • Use context clues to understand vocabulary • Use dictionary entries to select synonyms and accurate definitions • Skim for main idea and scan for important details • Organize information using an outline • Use outline to recall and summarize information	• Change adjectives to adverbs by adding the suffix: *-ly* • Recognize and use the suffixes: *-ion* and *-tion* • Identify and use parts of speech: nouns, verbs, adjectives, and adverbs • Use singular or plural nouns • Use correct verb tenses	• *Critical Thinking:* Understand inference; identify author's opinion and tone; express opinions supported with examples; draw conclusions; identify problems and suggest solutions • *Writing:* Write a summary; write an opinion paragraph supported with examples; write a journal entry • *Discussion:* Discuss opinions about alternative medicine
	Chapter 6 **Highs and Lows in Self-Esteem** *Page 96*	• Use visuals, title, chart, and questions to preview a reading • Analyze reading through True / False, Multiple Choice, and Short Answer questions • Use context clues to understand vocabulary • Use dictionary entries to select synonyms and accurate definitions • Scan for details • Take notes in a flowchart • Use notes to recall and summarize information	• Recognize and use the suffixes: *-tion* and *-ion* • Identify and use parts of speech: nouns and verbs • Use singular and plural nouns • Use correct verb tenses	• *Critical Thinking:* Critique author's conclusions; draw separate conclusions; create analogies • *Discussion:* Assert opinion; give advice; describe stages of self-esteem; generate solutions • *Writing:* Write a summary; take notes; support opinions with examples; write a journal entry

SKILLS

Unit	Chapter and Title	Reading Skills Focus	Structure Focus	Follow-up Activities Skills Focus
Unit 3 **Government and Education** *Page 117*	**Chapter 7** **The Federal System of Government** *Page 118*	• Preview reading • Analyze reading through True / False, Multiple Choice, and Short Answer questions • Use context clues to understand vocabulary • Use dictionary entries to select synonyms and accurate definitions • Scan for main idea and important details • Organize information using an outline • Use outline to recall and summarize information	• Recognize and use the suffixes: *-ce* and *-ment* • Identify and use parts of speech: nouns and verbs • Use singular and plural nouns • Use correct verb tenses	• *Critical Thinking:* Make inferences • *Discussion:* Compare types of governments; explain a branch of the U.S. government • *Writing:* Write a summary, take notes; fill out chart; describe a form of government; write a journal entry
	Chapter 8 **Teachers Are Key for Students** *Page 142*	• Use visuals, title, chart, and prereading questions to preview a reading • Analyze reading through True/False, Multiple Choice, and Short Answer questions • Use context clues to understand vocabulary • Use dictionary entries to select synonyms and accurate definitions • Scan for main ideas and details • Take notes in a flowchart • Use notes to recall and summarize information	• Change adjectives to adverbs by adding the suffix: *-ly* • Recognize and use the suffix: *-able* • Correctly identify and use parts of speech: verbs, adverbs and adjectives • Use correct verb tenses	• *Critical Thinking:* Make inferences about the reading; support opinions with examples; discuss author's perspective • *Discussion:* Discuss the impact of the environment on intelligence • *Writing:* Write a summary; write a list of ways to make yourself more intelligent; write a journal entry
	Chapter 9 **The Pursuit of Excellence** *Page 158*	• Use the title and prereading questions to preview reading • Analyze reading through True / False, Multiple Choice, and Short Answer questions • Use context clues to understand vocabulary • Use dictionary entries to select synonyms and accurate definitions • Scan for main ideas and details • Organize information using a chart • Use a chart to recall and summarize information	• Recognize and use the suffixes *-ity* and *-ce* • Identify and use parts of speech: adjectives and nouns	• *Critical Thinking:* Make inferences; make assumptions; analyze author's attitude and purpose • *Discussion:* Conduct survey and analyze resulting data; discuss advantages and disadvantages; make rules • *Writing:* Write a summary; use examples from reading to support opinion; compare and contrast advantages and disadvantages; write a letter

SKILLS

Unit	Chapter and Title	Reading Skills Focus	Structure Focus	Follow-up Activities Skills Focus
Unit 4 **Science and Technology** *Page 181*	**Chapter 10** **Antarctica: Whose Continent Is It Anyway?** *Page 182*	• Use visuals, title, chart, and prereading questions to preview a reading • Analyze reading through True / False, Multiple Choice, and Short Answer questions • Use context clues to understand vocabulary • Use dictionary entries to select synonyms and accurate definitions • Scan reading for main ideas and details • Take notes and organize information using an outline • Use outline to recall and summarize information	• Recognize and use the suffixes: *-ion, -tion*, and *-ment* • Identify and use parts of speech: nouns and verbs • Use singular and plural noun forms • Use correct verb tenses	• *Critical Thinking:* Analyze causes and effects; explain relationships between events • *Discussion:* Discuss rules; discuss places of interest • *Writing:* Write a summary; write guidelines; write an opinion paper; write a journal entry
	Chapter 11 **A Messenger from the Past** *Page 199*	• Use visuals, title, and prereading questions to preview a reading • Analyze reading through True / False, Multiple Choice, and Short Answer questions • Use context clues to understand vocabulary • Use dictionary entries to select synonyms and accurate definitions • Scan for main ideas and details • Take notes in a flowchart • Use notes to recall and summarize information	• Recognize and use the suffixes: *-ion* and *-tion* • Identify and use parts of speech: nouns and verbs • Use singular and plural noun forms • Use correct verb tenses	• *Critical Thinking:* Analyze the author's tone and purpose; support opinions with examples; make inferences • *Discussion:* Compare lists of questions • *Writing:* Write a summary, write a journal entry about an imagined historical scene
	Chapter 12 **Is Time Travel Possible?** *Page 218*	• Use visuals, title, and prereading questions to preview reading • Take a survey, and fill out a chart to activate background knowledge • Analyze reading through True / False, Multiple Choice, and Short Answer questions • Use context clues to understand vocabulary • Use dictionary entries to select synonyms and accurate definitions • Scan reading for the main idea • Organize information using a table or chart • Use a table or chart to recall and summarize information	• Recognize and use the suffixes: *-ance, -ence,* and *-al* • Identify and use parts of speech: adjectives, nouns, and verbs • Use correct verb tenses	• *Critical Thinking:* Analyze a proverb; support opinions with examples; speculate on reasons for results of survey • *Discussion:* Discuss and analyze results of a survey • *Writing:* Write a summary, write a composition about an imaginary experience; write a journal entry

• **Index of Key Words and Phrases** *Page 241*
• **Skills index** *Page 247*

Concepts for Today, Third Edition is a reading skills text intended for high-intermediate, college-bound students of English as a second or foreign language. The passages in this book have been selected from original articles published in a wide variety of periodicals, newspapers, and Web sites, thus allowing students the opportunity to read authentic materials from American publications. As they engage with the materials in each chapter of this book, students develop the kinds of extensive and intensive reading skills they will need to achieve academic success in English.

Concepts for Today is one in a series of five reading skills texts. The complete series has been designed to meet the needs of students from the beginning to the advanced levels and includes the following:

- *Reading for Today 1: Themes for Today*   beginning
- *Reading for Today 2: Insights for Today*   high beginning
- *Reading for Today 3: Issues for Today*   intermediate
- *Reading for Today 4: Concepts for Today*   high intermediate
- *Reading for Today 5: Topics for Today*   advanced

Concepts for Today, Third Edition consists of four thematic units. Each unit contains three chapters that deal with related subjects. However, for maximum flexibility in the classroom, each chapter is independent, entirely separate in content, from the other two chapters contained in that unit.

Organizing the chapters into thematic units provides for a natural recycling of content-specific vocabulary and concepts, and discipline-specific sentence structure and rhetorical patterns. It should be noted that although all three chapters in each unit are linked by theme, they can as easily be taught individually as in concert with one another. For the instructor who chooses to teach all three chapters in each unit, there is a unit-ending crossword puzzle and a discussion section that tie together the three related topics.

All of the chapters provide students with essential practice in the types of reading skills they will need in an academic environment. They require students not only to read text, but also to examine information from various kinds of charts, illustrations, and photographs. Furthermore, students are given the opportunity to speak and write about their own experiences, countries, and cultures in English, and to compare these experiences and ideas with those of people from the United States and other countries.

The initial exercise preceding each reading encourages the students to think about the ideas, facts, and vocabulary that will be presented in the passage. Discussing unit and chapter illustrations in class helps students visualize what they are going to read about and gives them cues for the new vocabulary they will encounter. The exercises that follow the reading passage are designed to develop and improve reading proficiency, including the ability to learn new vocabulary from context and to increase comprehension of English sentence structure. The exercises also help students to develop essential study skills such as note-taking and proper dictionary use. The follow-up activities give students the opportunity to master useful vocabulary encountered in the articles through discussion and group work, and lead the students to a comprehension of main ideas and specific information.

New to the Third Edition

Concepts for Today, Third Edition maintains the effective approach of the second edition with several significant improvements. This enhanced edition takes a more in-depth approach to vocabulary development and application by consistently introducing, practicing, and assessing vocabulary in context, while teaching valuable vocabulary-building skills that are recycled throughout the series.

Vocabulary development work includes a new *Vocabulary in Context* exercise in every chapter, which teaches the vocabulary from the reading along with related words and concepts. The *Word Forms* section now combines sentences into paragraphs to further develop the contextualized approach. Finally, *Word Partnership* boxes have been added from the *Collins COBUILD School Dictionary of American English* to increase students' ability to use language appropriately.

The third edition also contains three completely new chapters: "Junior Status: Sharing Dad's Name a Mixed Bag" in the Living in Society unit, "Laughter Is the Best Medicine for Your Heart" in the Health and Well-Being unit, and "Teachers Are Key for Students" in the Government and Education unit. In addition, new information has been added to "Messenger from the Past" to update the original article and keep it current.

Concepts for Today has an enhanced *Prereading Preparation* section, which provides thoughtful, motivating illustrations and activities. The third edition includes improved graphics art and photos, which are designed to facilitate students' understanding of the text they relate to. For an introduction to academic skills, *Information Organization* exercises include a main idea activity as well as outlines, charts, and flowcharts. This design takes into account students' different learning and organizational styles. For the development of critical thinking skills, the *Critical Thinking Strategies* section challenges students to apply the topic of the chapter to their own lives and draw conclusions.

All of these enhancements to ***Concepts for Today, Third Edition*** have been designed to help students improve their reading skills, build a stronger vocabulary, develop more interest in and confidence with text as they work through it, and thus be better prepared for the realities of academic work and the demands of the technical world.

How to Use This Book

Every chapter in this book consists of the following:

- Prereading Preparation
- Reading Passage
- Fact-Finding Exercise
- Reading Analysis
- Information Organization
- Information Organization Quiz and Summary
- Dictionary Skills
- Word Forms
- Critical Thinking Strategies
- Topics for Discussion and Writing
- Follow-Up Activities
- Cloze Quiz

Each unit features a *Unit Review*, consisting of a *Crossword Puzzle*, which incorporates vocabulary from all three chapters and a *Discussion* section, which ties together the related topics of the three chapters. There is an *Index of Key Words and Phrases* and the end of the book.

The format of each chapter in the book is consistent. Although each chapter can be done entirely in class, some exercises may be assigned for homework. This, of course, depends on the individual teacher's preference, as well as the availability of class time.

Prereading Preparation

The prereading activity is designed to stimulate student interest and provide preliminary vocabulary for the passage itself. The importance of prereading preparation should not be underestimated. Studies have shown the positive effect of prereading preparation in motivating students, activating background knowledge, and enhancing reading comprehension. Time should be spent describing and discussing the photographs and illustrations, as well as discussing the chapter title and the prereading questions. Furthermore, students should try to relate the topic to their own experiences and predict what they are going to read about.

The Reading Passage

Students will read the passage at least two times. They should be instructed to time themselves and to try to aim for a higher reading speed the second time they read the passage. They should also be encouraged to read *ideas*, not just words.

Fact-Finding Exercise

After the first reading, students will have a general idea of the information in the passage. The purpose of the *Fact-Finding Exercise* is to check students' overall comprehension. Students will read the *True/False* statements and check whether they are true or false. If a statement is false, students will rewrite the statement so that it is true. This activity can be done individually or in groups.

Reading Analysis

At this point, students have read the passage two or three times and should be familiar with the content of the reading. The *Reading Analysis Exercise* deals with vocabulary from context, transition words, punctuation clues, sentence structure, sentence comprehension, and pronoun referents. The teacher should review personal and relative pronouns before doing this section. This exercise may be assigned for homework, or it may be done in class individually or in groups, giving the students the opportunity to discuss their reasons for their answers.

Information Organization

In this exercise, students are asked to read the passage again, take notes, and organize the information they have just read. They may be asked to complete an outline, a table, or a flowchart. The teacher may want to review the concept of note taking before beginning the exercise. The outline, table, or flowchart can be sketched on the blackboard by the teacher or a student, and completed by individual students in front of the class. Variations can be discussed by the class as a group. It should be pointed out to the students that in American colleges, teachers often base their exams on the notes that students are expected to take during class lectures and that they, too, will be tested on *their* notes.

Information Organization Quiz and Summary

This quiz is based on the notes the students took in the *Information Organization* exercise. Students should be instructed to read the questions and then refer to their notes to answer them. They are also asked to write a summary of the article. The teacher may want to review how to summarize. This section can be a written assignment to be done as homework or as an actual test. Alternatively, it can be prepared in class and discussed.

Dictionary Skills

This exercise provides students with much needed practice in selecting the appropriate dictionary entry for an unknown word, depending on the context. In each of the first six chapters, the students are given entries from *Heinle's Newbury House Dictionary of American English, Fourth Edition* for several words from the reading in that chapter. The sentence containing the dictionary word is provided below the entry. The student selects the appropriate entry and writes the entry number and the definition or synonym into the sentence in the space provided. The students should write the answer in a grammatically correct form, since they may not always copy verbatim from the dictionary. In Chapters 7 to 12, the format is the same, but the entries are from *Merriam-Webster's Online Dictionary*. The students can work in pairs on this exercise and report back to the class. They should be prepared to justify their choices.

Word Forms

As an introduction to the *Word Form* exercises in this book, it is recommended that the teacher first review parts of speech, especially verbs, nouns, adjectives, and adverbs. The teacher should point out each word form's position in a sentence. Students will develop a sense for which part of speech is missing in a given sentence. The teacher should also point out clues to tense and number, and to whether an idea is affirmative or negative. The teacher can do the first item as an example with the students before the exercise. Each section has its own instructions, depending on the particular pattern that is being introduced. For example, in the section containing words that take *-tion* in the noun form, the teacher can explain that in this exercise the student will look at the two types of words that use the suffixes *-ion* or *-tion* in their noun form. (1) Some words simply add *-ion* to the verb: *suggest / suggestion;* if the word ends in *-e,* the *-e* is dropped first, and *-tion* is added: *produce / production;* (2) other words drop the final *-e* and add *-ation: examine / examination.* This exercise is very effective when done in pairs. After students have a working knowledge of this type of exercise, it can be assigned for homework.

Word Partnership boxes selected from the *Collins COBUILD School Dictionary of American English* are used to reinforce and enhance this section. These boxes help students notice which words typically partner, or collocate, with one or two of the words from the *Word Forms* section. The teacher can use the examples given in the directions for each chapter's *Word Forms* section and the words in the *Word Partnership* boxes at the end of the section to see that students understand the exercise.

Critical Thinking Strategies

The goal of the exercise is for students to form their own ideas and opinions on aspects of the topic discussed. Students refer back to parts of the article and think about the implications of the information or comments it contains. There are also questions about the author's purpose and tone. Students can work on these questions as individual writing exercises or in a small group discussion activity.

Topics for Discussion and Writing

In this section, students are encouraged to use the information and vocabulary from the passage, both orally and in writing. The writing assignment may be done in class or at home. There is a *Write in your journal* suggestion for every chapter. Students should be encouraged to keep a journal. The teacher may want to read and respond to the students' journal entries, but not correct them.

Follow-Up Activities

This section contains various activities appropriate to the information in the passages. Some activities are designed for pair and small-group work. Students are encouraged to use the information and vocabulary from the passages both orally and in writing. Some activities, such as surveys, prompt students to interact with native English speakers to collect data in the "real world," which they chart or graph and then discuss in class. For other activity types, the teacher may assign certain questions or the entire activity as an at-home or in-class assignment.

Cloze Quiz

The *Cloze Quiz* tests not only vocabulary but also sentence structure and comprehension in general. The quiz is a modified version of the reading passage itself, with 20 items to be completed. At the top of the answer page, students are given the 20 words to be used in the blank spaces. The quiz is placed at the end of each chapter. The quizzes can be done either as a test or as a group assignment.

Unit Review

At the end of every three chapters, students have a chance to review the material they have been working with. The *Unit Review* consists of two sections: *Crossword Puzzle* and *Discussion.* These two activities consolidate the vocabulary and content from the three chapters in the unit.

Crossword Puzzle

The *Unit Crossword Puzzle* in each chapter is based on the vocabulary used in that chapter. Students can go over the puzzle orally if pronunciation practice with letters is needed. The teacher can have students spell out their answers in addition to pronouncing the word itself. Students invariably enjoy doing crossword puzzles. They are a fun way to reinforce the vocabulary presented in the various exercises in each chapter, and require students to pay attention to correct spelling. At the same time, students need to connect the meaning of a word and think of the word itself. If the teacher prefers, students can do the crossword puzzle on their own or with a partner in their free time, or after they have completed an in-class assignment and are waiting for the rest of their classmates to finish.

Discussion

This section contains questions that help students connect the related topics in the three chapters for that unit. The questions may be discussed in class or assigned as written homework.

Index of Key Words and Phrases

At the back of the book is the *Index of Key Words and Phrases*. This section contains words and phrases from all the chapters for easy reference. *The Index of Key Words and Phrases* may be useful to students to help them locate words they need or wish to review.

We are thankful to everyone at Heinle, especially Sherrise Roehr, Tom Jefferies, Laura Le Dréan, and Maryellen Killeen. As always, we are very appreciative of the ongoing encouragement from our family and friends.

L.C.S. and N.N.M.

UNIT

1

Living in Society

1 CHAPTER

The Paradox of Happiness
by Diane Swanbrow
Psychology Today

Prereading Preparation

1. **a.** In groups of three, write a definition of **happy.** Write what it means to be happy. On the board, compare your definitions with the definitions of the other groups in the class.

   b. Do the same for **unhappy.**

   c. Compare your class explanations of **happy** and **unhappy.** Are they opposites? Is there a relationship between happiness and unhappiness?

2. What makes you happy? What makes you unhappy?

3. **a.** Are you a happy person?

   b. Do you come from a happy family?

4. Do you think your environment can cause you to be happy or unhappy? Explain your answer.

5. Look at the title of this article. What is a **paradox?** Why might there be a paradox involving happiness and unhappiness?

The Paradox of Happiness

It's plain common sense—the more happiness you feel, the less unhappiness you experience. It's plain common sense, but it's not true. Recent research reveals that happiness and unhappiness are not really flip sides of the same emotion. They are two distinct feelings that, coexisting, rise and fall independently.

"You'd think that the higher a person's level of unhappiness, the lower their level of happiness and vice versa," says Edward Diener, a University of Illinois professor of psychology who has done much of the new work on positive and negative emotions. But when Diener and other researchers measure people's average levels of happiness and unhappiness, they often find little relationship between the two.

The recognition that feelings of happiness and unhappiness can coexist much like love and hate in a close relationship may offer valuable clues on how to lead a happier life. It suggests, for example, that changing or avoiding things that make you miserable may well make you less miserable but probably won't make you any happier. That advice is backed up by an extraordinary series of studies which indicate that a genetic predisposition for unhappiness may run in certain families. On the other hand, researchers have found, happiness doesn't appear to be anyone's heritage. The capacity for joy is a talent you develop largely for yourself.

Psychologists have settled on a working definition of the feeling—happiness is a sense of subjective well-being. They've also begun to find out who's happy, who isn't, and why. To date, the research hasn't found a simple recipe for a happy life, but it has discovered some of the actions and attitudes that seem to bring people closer to that most desired of feelings.

In a number of studies of identical and fraternal twins, researchers have examined the role genetics plays in happiness and unhappiness. The work suggests that although no one is really born to be happy, sadness may run in families.

In one University of Southern California study, psychologist Laura Baker and colleagues compared 899 individuals who had taken several commonly used tests for happiness and unhappiness. The men and women included 105 pairs of identical and fraternal twins as well as grandparents, parents, and young adult offspring from more than 200 other families.

"Family members," Baker reports, "resembled each other more in their levels of unhappiness than in their levels of happiness." Furthermore, identical twins were much closer than fraternal twins in unhappiness, a finding that implies a genetic component.

In a study at the University of Minnesota, twins (some raised together and others who had grown up apart) were tested for a wide range of personality traits. In terms of happiness—defined as the capacity to enjoy life—identical twins who were separated soon after birth were considerably less alike than twins raised together. But when it came to *unhappiness*, the twins raised apart—some without contact for as long as 64 years—were as similar as those who'd grown up together.

Why is unhappiness less influenced by environment? When we're happy we are more responsive to people and keep up connections better than when we're feeling sad.

This doesn't mean, however, that some people are born to be sad and that's that. Genes may predispose one to unhappiness, but disposition can be influenced by personal choice. You can increase your happiness through your own actions.

In a series of experiments by psychologists John Reich and Alex Zautra at Arizona State University, they asked students to select their favorite activities from a list of everyday pleasures—things like going to a movie, talking with friends and playing cards.

Then the researchers instructed some of the subjects to increase the number of favorite activities they participated in for one month (the other participants in the study served as controls and did not vary their activity level). Results: Those who did more of the things they enjoyed were happier than those who didn't. The conclusion, then, is that the pleasure we get from life is largely ours to control.

Fact-Finding Exercise

Read the passage again. Then read the following statements. Scan the article quickly to see if they are True (T) or False (F). If a statement is false, rewrite it so that it is true.

1 _____ T _____ F   The feeling of unhappiness may be genetic.

_____

2 _____ T _____ F   There is a strong relationship between levels of happiness and unhappiness in a person.

_____

3 _____ T _____ F   Researchers have found that happiness is inherited.

_____

4 _____ T _____ F   Unhappiness is less influenced by environment than it is by genetics.

_____

5 _____ T _____ F   It is impossible to increase your happiness.

_____

6 _____ T _____ F   We can control our own happiness.

_____

Reading Analysis

Read each question carefully. Circle the number or letter of the correct answer, or write your answer in the space provided.

1 Read lines 6 and 7: "You'd think that the higher a person's level of unhappiness, the lower their level of happiness and **vice versa.**"

    a. **Vice versa** means that

        1. the lower a person's level of unhappiness, the higher their level of happiness
        2. the higher a person's level of unhappiness, the higher their level of happiness
        3. the lower a person's level of unhappiness, the lower their level of happiness

    b. **Vice versa** means

        1. the same thing is true
        2. the reverse is true

2 Read lines 9–11. What does **the two** refer to?

    a. Diener and other researchers
    b. Positive and negative emotions
    c. Happiness and unhappiness

3 Read lines 14–16. **Miserable** means

_____

4 Read lines 16–18.

    a. What does **back up** mean?

        1. Go behind
        2. Write
        3. Support

    b. "Studies indicate that a genetic predisposition for unhappiness may run in certain families. **On the other hand,** happiness doesn't appear to be anyone's heritage." This sentences means that

        1. the tendency to be unhappy is inherited, but happiness is not
        2. the tendency to be unhappy is inherited, and happiness is, too
        3. the tendency to be happy is inherited, but unhappiness is not

   c. Complete the following sentence with the appropriate choice: John is happy being a student in another country because he can study what he wants. **On the other hand,** he is unhappy because

      1. he is far from his family and friends
      2. he knows people from many different countries
      3. his English skills are improving

5 Read lines 39–45.

   a. According to the University of Minnesota study, what is **happiness?**

      _____

   b. How do you know?

      _____

   c. Why is the phrase **some without contact for as long as 64 years** separated from the rest of the sentence by dashes (—)?

      _____

6 Read lines 49–50. **That's that** means:

   a. some people are born to be sad, and there is nothing they can do to change the situation
   b. some people are born to be sad, and they don't think about it
   c. some people are born to be sad, and some people are born to be happy

7 Read lines 53–56.

   a. What are some of the everyday pleasures on the list that the students read?

      _____

   b. How do you know?

      _____

8 Read lines 59–61.

   a. **Those who didn't** refers to

      1. the students who didn't participate in the study
      2. the students who didn't increase the number of favorite activities
      3. the students who didn't become happier

   b. In this context, **largely** means

      1. hugely
      2. completely
      3. mostly

Information Organization

Read the article again. Underline what you think are the main ideas. Then scan the article and complete the following outline, using the sentences that you have underlined to help you. You will use this outline later to answer specific questions about the article.

I. What New Research Shows about Happiness and Unhappiness

   A. *The tendency to feel unhappy may be in your genes*

   B. _____

   C. _____

II. Studies on the Role of Genetics in Happiness and Unhappiness

   A. University of Southern California

      1. Subjects:

         899 individuals (identical and fraternal twins, grandparents, parents and

         young adult offspring)

      2. Results:

         _____

      3. Conclusion:

         _____

   B. University of Minnesota

      1. Subjects:

         _____

      2. Results:
         a. In terms of happiness,

         _____

         b. In terms of unhappiness,

         _____

      3. Conclusion:

         _____

III. The Implications of the Studies on Happiness and Unhappiness

    A. *Genes only predispose a person to unhappiness* _____

    B. _____

IV. Arizona State University Experiment on Happiness

    A. Subjects: _____

    B. Experiment:

        1. _____

        2. _____

    C. Result: _____

    D. Conclusion: *The pleasure we get from life is largely ours to control* _____

Information Organization Quiz and Summary

Read each question carefully. Use your notes to answer the questions. Do not refer back to the text. When you are finished, write a brief summary of the article.

1 What do researchers believe about happiness and unhappiness?

_____

_____

_____

2 Describe the study done at the University of Southern California. Who did researchers study? What did the researchers learn?

_____

_____

_____

3 Describe the experiment done at Arizona State University. Who did the researchers study? How? What was the result of the study?

_____

_____

_____

4 According to this article, how can we increase our happiness?

_____

_____

_____

Summary

_____

_____

_____

_____

_____

_____

Dictionary Skills

Read the dictionary entry for each word. Then look at how the word is used in the sentence. Write the number of the correct definition and the synonym or meaning in the space provided. The first one has been done as an example.

1   **distinct** *adj.* **1** clear, easy to see: *Medical care has made a distinct improvement in his health.* **2** separate, different: *Those two types of birds are quite distinct (from each other).* *–adv.* **distinctly.**

Happiness and unhappiness are not really flip sides of the same emotion.

They are two **(2) separate / different** feelings that, coexisting, rise and fall independently.

2   **close** *adj.* **1** with little space between, nearby: *Her chair is close to the wall.* **2** near in time: *It's close to 5:00.* **3** very friendly: *They are a close family with a few close friends.* **4** with air that is not fresh and is usu. too warm: *It is very close in this room; let's open a window.* **5** with strict control: *The doctor put her patient under close observation.* **6** **a close call: a.** s.t. that is difficult to judge: *The two runners crossed the finish line together, so who won was a close call (or) too close to call.* **b.** a narrow escape from danger or death: *The speeding taxi nearly hit him; that was a close call (or) a close shave.*

Feelings of love and hate can coexist in relationships that are very

(   ) _____ , for example, the relationship between a husband and wife.

3   **lead** *v.* **led, leading, leads** **1** [T] to go first to show the way: *She led the visitors on a tour through the museum.* **2** [I;T] to be ahead of, in front of: *He leads the others in the race by several meters.* **3** [T] to direct, control: *She led the orchestra (the discussion, the team, etc.).* **4** [I] to be a route to: *That road leads to the river.* **5** [T] to experience, live (a life): *He leads an exciting life.* **6** [T] to influence or cause (s.o. to do s.t.): *Her expression led me to believe there was some problem.*

Understanding our feelings helps us (   ) _____ lives that are happier.

[C]—Countable (noun); [U]—Uncountable (noun); s.o.—someone, s.t.—something; (*syn.*)—synonym; *n.*—noun; *v.*—verb; I—Intransitive; T—Transitive

Word Forms

In English, verbs can change to nouns in several ways. Some verbs become nouns by adding the suffixes *-ion* or *-tion,* for example, *suggest (v.), suggestion (n.).*

Complete each sentence with the correct form of the words on the left. Be careful of spelling changes. **Use the simple present tense of the verbs, in the affirmative form. Use the singular form of the nouns.**

indicate *(v.)*

indication *(n.)*

1 Traffic signals have three signals. A red light

_____ *stop,* and a green light means *go.*

A yellow, or amber, light is an _____ that

the light is going to become red. It means *prepare to*

stop.

participate *(v.)*

participation *(n.)*

2 Many college students _____ in sports

such as soccer, tennis, and swimming to keep in shape.

In fact, regular _____ in a sport is also a

good way to make friends.

define *(v.)*

definition *(n.)*

3 I don't understand what *influence* means. Can you

give me a simple _____? Most people

_____ *influence* as the power to affect a

person or an event.

recognize *(v.)*

recognition *(n.)*

4 Joan has an incredible memory for faces. She actually

_____ people that she hasn't seen for

years. Her powers of _____ are well

known among her friends.

imply (v.)

implication (n.)

5 Diane Swanbrow _____ that many "opposite" feelings may not really be opposites at all. This is an interesting _____ . Are *like* and *dislike* not really opposites?

In English, verbs can change to nouns in several ways. Some verbs become nouns by adding the suffixes -*ance* or -*ence,* for example, *insist (v.), insistence (n.).*
  Complete each sentence with the correct form of the words on the left. **Use the simple present tense of the verbs, in either the affirmative or the negative form. Use the singular form of the nouns.**

appear (v.)

appearance (n.)

1 Peter _____ to be very unhappy. His sad _____ makes me wonder what's wrong.

avoid (v.)

avoidance (n.)

2 Susan _____ going to a doctor even when she's very sick. Her _____ of doctors is not good. She should see one when she's ill.

assist (v)

assistance (n.)

3 Can you help me for a moment? I need your _____ . This box is too heavy for me to pick up by myself. If you _____ me, I won't be able to pick up the box.

resemble (v.)

resemblance (n.)

4 Michael _____ his mother at all. She has blond hair and blue eyes. He has dark hair and brown eyes. Michael has a much stronger _____ to his father, who has dark hair and brown eyes, too.

exist (v.)

existence (n.)

5 Some people believe in the _____ of life in other solar systems. I also think that life _____ on other planets besides Earth.

perform *(v.)*

performance *(n.)*

6 The actor in the new play _____ very well in all his appearances. Consequently, I am looking forward to his first _____ tonight.

Word Partnership	Use *existence* with:
v.	**come into** existence, **deny the** existence
adj.	**continued** existence, **daily** existence, **everyday** existence

Word Partnership	Use *perform* with:
n.	perform **miracles**, perform **tasks**
adj.	**able to** perform
v.	**continue to** perform
adv.	perform **well**

Critical Thinking Strategies

Read each question carefully, and write a response. Remember that there is no one correct answer. Your response depends on what **you** think.

1 According to this article, feelings of happiness and unhappiness can coexist. Similarly, love and hate can coexist in a close relationship. How can you explain such conflicting feelings in a relationship? Do you think a person can be happy and sad at the same time? Explain your answer.

_____

_____

_____

_____

_____

2 The author mentions several studies of identical and fraternal twins. These studies conclude that sadness may run in families. Why do you think researchers like to study twins rather than other brothers and sisters? Why do you think researchers compare identical twins who grew up together with identical twins who grew up apart?

_____

_____

_____

_____

_____

3 According to the University of Southern California study, "identical twins were much closer than fraternal twins in unhappiness, a finding that implies a genetic component." Why do you think identical twins were more alike than fraternal twins were?

_____

_____

_____

_____

_____

4 The author describes two studies, one at the University of Southern California and one at the University of Minnesota. She also describes an experiment at Arizona State University. What do you think is the difference between doing a study and doing an experiment?

_____

_____

_____

_____

_____

5　What do you think the author believes about happiness and unhappiness? Does she believe they are opposites? What do you think her opinion is?

_____

_____

_____

Topics for Discussion and Writing

1　What was the happiest time in your life? Why was it a happy time? Write a composition about this and describe what it was that made you feel happy.

2　At the end of the article, the author states, "The conclusion, then, is that the pleasure we get from life is largely ours to control." Do you agree with her? Can we control our pleasure in life? Discuss this with your classmates.

3　Work with a partner. How important is happiness in your life? Are there other things that are more important to you than happiness? Make a list of what is important in your life, and compare it to your classmate's list. Then choose the one thing that is most important in your life, and write about it. Give examples to show why it is so important to you.

4　**Write in your journal.** Researchers think that sadness runs in families. Do you agree or disagree? Explain your opinion, and give examples to support your ideas.

Follow-Up Activities

1 According to the author, Diane Swanbrow, there are seven steps to happiness:

1. Develop loving relationships with other people.
2. Work hard at what you like.
3. Be helpful to other people.
4. Make the time to do whatever makes you happy.
5. Stay in good physical condition.
6. Be organized, but be flexible in case something unexpected comes up.
7. Try to keep things in perspective.

Alone or with a classmate, examine these seven steps. Put them in order of importance to you. For example, the most important step to happiness is number one; the least important step is number seven. Compare your ordered list with your classmates' lists.

2 Work with your classmates as a group.

a. Make a list of activities that people enjoy (e.g., going to the movies, listening to music, etc.).

b. Take a survey to see which activities each classmate enjoys. Write the results on the board.

c. Refer to the Activity Chart on page 18. Add to the chart the activities that you listed on the board. Keep a personal record of the activities you do for the rest of the term. Use each box on the right for a weekly check.

d. At the end of the term, do an in-class survey to find out if the people who increased the number of favorite activities that they participated in actually feel happier. Do your results support or disprove the Arizona State University findings?

ACTIVITY CHART

Activity / Week										
read										
watch TV										
write letters										
listen to music										
take a walk										
go bicycling										

J Cloze Quiz

Complete the passage with words from the list. Use each word only once.

advice	found	largely	relationship
appear	genetic	less	researchers
avoiding	happier	level	run
close	higher	miserable	studies
emotions	joy	recognition	unhappiness

"You'd think that the _____ (1) a person's level of unhappiness, the lower their _____ (2) of happiness and vice versa," says Edward Diener, who has done much of the new work on positive and negative _____ (3) . But when Diener and other _____ (4) measure people's average levels of happiness and unhappiness, they often find little _____ (5) between the two.

The _____ (6) that feelings of happiness and _____ (7) can coexist much like love and hate in a _____ (8) relationship may offer valuable clues on how to lead a _____ (9) life. It suggests, for example, that changing or _____ (10) things that make you _____ (11) may well make you _____ (12) miserable but probably won't make you any happier. That _____ (13) is backed up by an extraordinary series of _____ (14) which indicate that a _____ (15) predisposition for unhappiness may _____ (16) in certain families. On the other hand, researchers have _____ (17) , happiness doesn't _____ (18) to be anyone's heritage. The capacity for _____ (19) is a talent you develop _____ (20) for yourself.

Junior Status: Sharing Dad's Name a Mixed Bag

by Melissa Dahl, *MSNBC.com*

CHAPTER

José Martinez and José Martinez, Jr.

Prereading Preparation

1. Look at the picture and answer the questions.
   a. Who are these people? _____
   b. Why do they have the same names?

      _____

   c. What does **Jr.** mean? _____

2. Were you named after someone? If so, who?

   _____

3. In your culture, is it common for a father and son to have the same name? Why or why not?

   _____

4. Look at the title of the chapter. What does it mean?
   a. Sharing dad's name has a number of disadvantages.
   b. Sharing dad's name has a number of advantages.
   c. Sharing dad's name has advantages and disadvantages.

Junior Status: Sharing Dad's Name a Mixed Bag

1   When he was a kid, being José Martinez, Jr., was often a little annoying. He was always Little José to his dad's Big, and he could never tell which José callers wanted. But as this particular Junior's grown up, his name, once a source of annoyance and confusion, now makes him proud. "I look at my dad now, and

5   I can say with complete certainty that if I grow to be half the man that he is, I'll have lived a good life," Martinez says.

    For dads who name their sons after themselves, it can be a very public way to let the world know: This is my son. This one belongs to me. It can also be a mother's way of honoring her hubby. "When they're giving their name to a

10   child, they're giving an endorsement, or approval," says behavioral psychologist Matt Wallaert. He's named after his dad and says he's closer to his namesake than his brother is. "It does provide the early chance for this strong bonding."

    But the American Junior—not to mention IIIs, IVs and Vs—is something of a dying breed, says Cleveland Evans, a psychology professor at Bellevue University

15   in Nebraska who specializes in omnastics, or the study of names. "The percentage of juniors has been going down in American culture in general over the last 40 years at least," says Evans, adding that in the Hispanic community it remains a popular naming trend. "I think that it's become more of a value for people to have every child have an individual name," Evans continues. "There's more emphasis

20   on individualism, there's less pressure to carry on family names than there used to be, and there's much more worry about the inconvenience of what happens when you have two people of the same name in the same family."

    In the latest inconvenience for 19-year-old Martinez, he arrived for his freshman year at Loyola Marymount University in Los Angeles only to discover

25   that it was José Senior, not Junior, who was registered for all of his classes. (He knew because in this family, José Junior has a middle name; José Senior does not.) It was easy enough to change, he says, but he did spend half his freshman year with his dad's name on his ID card.

    "We now have a culture where a lot of young parents don't want their child to

30   have the same name as any other child in the class at school," Evans says. "You see posts on baby name discussion boards asking, 'Gee, is it OK for me to name my child the same name as my second cousin who lives across the country?' . . . Nowadays parents feel your child has to have a name that differentiates him from everyone else in the population—including the parents."

35   Carleton Warren Kendrick, Jr. cut the suffix from his name when he left his tiny Massachusetts town for Harvard at age 18. "It wasn't a slam against my

dad," says Kendrick, now a Boston-area family therapist. "I was not only trying to be a young man with my own personal identity . . . I needed to create more who I was apart from being my dad's son." For Kendrick, even though he ultimately ended his juniorship, he says that as a kid, sharing his dad's name helped forge a tight bond between the two. "I wanted to be like him," he recalls.

A dad who names his child after himself might be more invested in that child's life, says Frank McAndrew, a professor of psychology at Knox College in Illinois who has researched namesaking. He points out one study that found that sons who share their dads' first names had fewer behavioral problems.

As John Garcia III watches his 1-year-old son John Garcia IV ("Baby John") grow up, he hopes he can show him only the best examples of what being John Garcia means, as his father and grandfather did for him. Of course, most fathers are aware of the need to be a good example to their son—but that obligation is underscored when you're calling the kid by your own name, Garcia says. "You hope he gains your characteristics, your traits, over the years—the good ones, anyway," says Garcia, who lives in Cyprus, California (as does John Garcia, Jr.).

Growing up as a girl named Sam, 54-year-old Samuella Becker can relate. Her father, Samuel, died of cancer four months before she was born in 1954. Her mother decided to honor his memory by giving their girl a feminized version of his name. "Growing up in Akron, Ohio, it was a little bit different from today, when everyone wants a different, unique name," says Becker, who lives in Manhattan. "Now there are a lot of female versions of male names. But Samuella, of course, never caught on."

She remembers a childhood of being assigned to boys' gym classes, of being accused by a substitute teacher of sitting in the wrong seat on purpose and of desperately wishing for a glamorous, feminine name like Diana. But she's learned to love her name for its uniqueness, and for giving her a piece of a father she never met.

Fact-Finding Exercise

Read the passage again. Then read the following statements. Scan the article quickly to see if they are True (T) or False (F). If a statement is false, rewrite it so that it is true.

1 _____ T _____ F   When José Martinez, Jr. was young, he didn't always like having the same name as his father.

_____

2 _____ T _____ F   José Martinez, Jr. is proud to have his father's name now.

_____

3 _____ T _____ F   Every year, more Americans give their sons the same name as their fathers.

_____

4 _____ T _____ F   Many young parents want their children to have names that are different from their classmates' names.

_____

5 _____ T _____ F   Carleton Warren Kendrick, Jr., changed his name because he doesn't like his father.

_____

6 _____ T _____ F   Frank McAndrew believes that fathers are more interested in their sons if they have the same name.

_____

7 _____ T _____ F   When Samuella Becker was a child, she enjoyed having an unusual name.

_____

Reading Analysis

Read each question carefully. Circle the number or letter of the correct answer, or write your answer in the space provided.

1 Read lines 3–5. José Martinez, Jr. says, "I look at my dad now, and I can say with complete certainty that if I grow to be half the man that he is, I'll have lived a good life." This means that he has

   a. a positive opinion of his father

   b. a negative opinion of his father

   c. a confusing opinion of his father

2 Read lines 8–12.

   a. Hubby means

      1. father

      2. son

      3. husband

   b. Which word is a synonym for **endorsement?**

      _____

   c. How do you know?

      _____

   d. Who is Matt Wallaert's **namesake?**

      1. Matt Wallaert's brother

      2. Matt Wallaert's father

      3. Matt Wallaert's son

   e. Matt Wallaert has a strong bond with

      1. his brother

      2. his father

      3. his son

   f. Closer to means to

      1. have a stronger bond with

      2. live much nearer to

      3. be much nicer to

3   **a.** In lines 13–14, **something of a dying breed** means it is

      1. very popular

      2. a little popular

      3. no longer popular

b. In line 15, **omnastics** refers to

_____

4 Read lines 19–22.

   a. **There's more emphasis on individualism** means

      1. parents want their children to be unique and different
      2. parents want their children to be the same as other children
      3. parents only want to have one child

   b. **There's less pressure to carry on family names than there used to be** means

      1. more people today think it's important to give their children family names
      2. fewer people today think it's important to give their children family names

5 Read lines 23–25. What was **the latest inconvenience for 19-year-old Martinez?**

   a. He forgot to register for his classes.
   b. His father's name was on his college I.D.
   c. His father took the same classes as he did.

6 Read lines 35–36. **Carleton Warren Kendrick, Jr. cut the suffix from his name when he left his tiny Massachusetts town for Harvard at age 18.** This sentence means that Carleton changed his name to

   a. Carleton Warren Kendrick
   b. Carleton Warren Kendrick, Jr.
   c. Carleton Kendrick, Jr.

7 In line 41, **forge a tight bond** means

   a. build a strong relationship
   b. choose a different name
   c. separate from someone

8 Read lines 42–44. **Frank McAndrew . . . has researched namesaking. Namesaking** refers to

   a. doing some research
   b. having behavioral problems
   c. giving a child the same name as his or her father

9 Read lines 55–56. Why did Samuella Becker's mother give her an unusual name?

   a. She wanted her daughter to be unique.
   b. She wanted to honor Samuella's father, who died before she was born.
   c. She wanted her daughter to have a difficult time in school.

Information Organization

C

Read the article again. Underline the names of all the people in the reading. Pay attention to what each person thinks. Then fill in the following chart about the people in the reading. The first one is done as an example.

Name of person	What is his or her experience with namesaking?	What does he or she think about namesaking?
1. José Martinez, Jr.	He was named for his father.	When he was a child, it was confusing. Now he feels proud.
2.		
3.		
4.		
5.		
6.		
7.		

UNIT 1   LIVING IN SOCIETY

D Information Organization
Quiz and Summary

Read each question carefully. Use your notes and the chart on the previous page to answer the questions. Do not refer back to the text. When you are finished, write a brief summary of the article.

1 What are some reasons people name their children after their fathers?

_____

_____

_____

_____

2 What are some reasons people don't name their children after their fathers?

_____

_____

_____

_____

3 What are some problems that namesakes (children who share their father's name) sometimes have? Give examples.

_____

_____

_____

_____

4 Is namesaking in the United States increasing or decreasing? Why?

_____

_____

_____

_____

Summary

_____

_____

_____

_____

E Dictionary Skills

Read the dictionary entry for each word. Then look at how the word is used in the sentence. Write the number of the correct definition and the synonym or meaning in the space provided. **Be sure to use the correct form of the verbs and nouns.**

1 | **honor** *v.* [T] **1** to praise, give recognition to: *She was honored by the mayor with a good citizenship award.* **2** to show respect: *The son honors his parents by caring for them.* **3** to fulfill a promise or obligation: *She honored her student loans by paying them.*

It can also be a mother's way of (   ) _____ her hubby.

2 | **invest** *v.* **1** [I;T] to put money into a business idea or activity in the hope of making more money if it is successful: *We invested in a hamburger restaurant and became rich when it expanded to Europe.* **2** [T] to put effort (time, money, energy, etc.) into s.t.: *We invested a lot in our garden, and now we have flowers and vegetables.*

A dad who names his child after himself might (   )

_____ that child's life, says Frank McAndrew.

3 | **underscore** *v.* [T] -scored, -scoring, -scores **1** to underline: *He underscored an important idea in the report with a pen.* **2** to emphasize, tell how important s.t. is: *She underscored her desire to cooperate with the police by going with them.*

Most fathers are aware of the need to be a good example to their son—but

that obligation (   ) _____ when you're calling the kid by your own name.

Word Forms

PART 1

In English, verbs change to nouns in several ways. Some verbs become nouns by adding the suffixes *-ion* or *-tion*, for example, *correct (v.), correction (n.)*.

Complete each sentence with a correct form of the words on the left. **Use the simple present or past tense of the verb in either the affirmative or the negative form. Use the singular form of the nouns.**

confuse *(v.)*
confusion *(n.)*

1 On the first day of class, the new school _____ the students. They didn't know their way around the campus. However, the _____ didn't last long, and the students felt more comfortable the next day.

discuss *(v.)*
discussion *(n.)*

2 Yesterday Sophia had a long _____ with her parents. They _____ where she would go to college, and what she wanted to study.

populate *(v.)*
population *(n.)*

3 The _____ of the United States increases every year, but the largest number of people _____ cities on the East and West coasts.

register *(v.)*
registration *(n.)*

4 Julio always _____ for his classes early because the lines for _____ are shorter at that time.

specialize *(v.)*
specialization *(n.)*

5 Dr. Hu's _____ is in heart disease. She _____ in kidney or lung illnesses.

PART 2

In English, the verb and noun forms of some words are the same, for example, *help (n.)* and *help (v.)*.

Complete each sentence with the correct form of the word on the left. **Use the correct tense of the verb in either the affirmative or the negative form. Use the singular or plural form of the noun. In addition, indicate whether you are using the noun or verb form by circling *v.* or *n.*.**

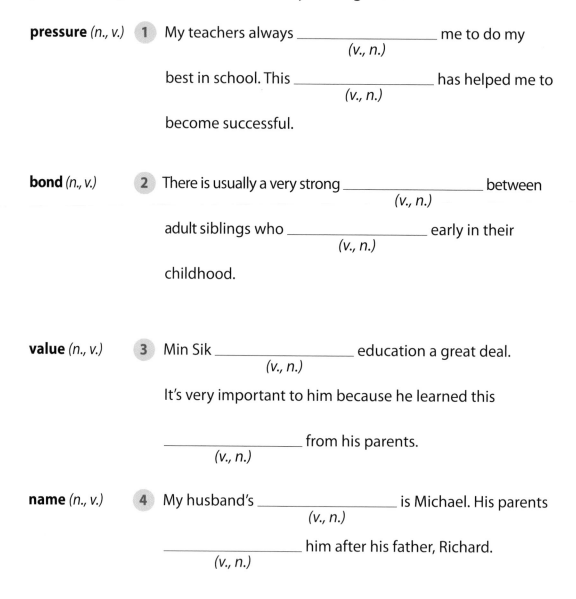

pressure *(n., v.)* **1** My teachers always _____ me to do my
(v., n.)

best in school. This _____ has helped me to
(v., n.)

become successful.

bond *(n., v.)* **2** There is usually a very strong _____ between
(v., n.)

adult siblings who _____ early in their
(v., n.)

childhood.

value *(n., v.)* **3** Min Sik _____ education a great deal.
(v., n.)

It's very important to him because he learned this

_____ from his parents.
(v., n.)

name *(n., v.)* **4** My husband's _____ is Michael. His parents
(v., n.)

_____ him after his father, Richard.
(v., n.)

worry *(n., v.)* **5** Margaret _____ that she had failed her exam.
(v., n.)

However, her _____ was not necessary—she
(v., n.)

easily passed the test.

Critical Thinking Strategies

Read each question carefully, and write a response. Remember that there is no one correct answer. Your response depends on what **you** think.

1 Frank McAndrew, a professor of psychology at Knox College in Illinois, found that sons who share their dads' first names had fewer behavioral problems. What do you think might be a reason for this?

_____

_____

_____

2 In the article, Cleveland Evans states that, "It's become more of a value for people to have every child have an individual name," and not to be named after a family member. At the same time, when people have children, they often pick names that are popular at the time, as you can see in the chart on page 33. Do you think this is a contradiction? Why do people often choose popular names instead of truly individual names for their children?

_____

_____

_____

Topics for Discussion and Writing

1 What is your opinion about namesaking? Is it a good idea for a child to have the same name as his father? Why or why not?

2 Imagine that you have a child. What will you name it? Will you name it after someone, or will you give your child a different name? What are your reasons?

3 The article discusses naming boys after their fathers, and even one girl who was named after her father. Parents sometimes name their daughters after their mothers. How might this practice have an influence on the daughter?

4 **Write in your journal.** Tell why you have the name you have. Describe what meaning it has, if you know. Do you like your name? Would you rather have been given a different name? What name would you have preferred? Why?

Follow-Up Activities

1 Below is a chart of the top ten names for children in the United States. Do a search on the Internet. What are the most popular names for children in your culture? Present your list to your class.

TOP 10 NAMES FOR 2009		
Rank	Male name	Female name
1	Jacob	Emma
2	Michael	Isabella
3	Ethan	Emily
4	Joshua	Madison
5	Daniel	Ava
6	Alexander	Olivia
7	Anthony	Sophia
8	William	Abigail
9	Christopher	Elizabeth
10	Matthew	Chloe
Note: Rank 1 is the most popular, rank 2 is the next most popular, and so forth.		

2 Different cultures have different ways of naming children. Think about how children are named in your culture. As a class, complete the following chart. Put your answers together by country, culture, religion, etc., depending on the way children are traditionally named.

Country, culture, etc.	How children are named

J

Cloze Quiz

Complete the passage with words from the list. Use each word once.

American	down	name	specializes
annoying	endorsement	namesake	strong
belongs	honoring	popular	used
certainty	inconvenience	pressure	value
confusion	individual	professor	world

When he was a kid, being José Martinez, Jr., was often a little

_____. He was always Little José to his dad's Big, and he

(1)

could never tell which José callers wanted. But as this particular Junior's

grown up, his name, once a source of annoyance and _____,

(2)

now makes him proud. "I look at my dad now, and I can say with complete

_____ that if I grow to be half the man that he is, I'll have lived

(3)

a good life," Martinez says.

For dads who _____ their sons after themselves, it can

(4)

be a very public way to let the _____ know: This is my

(5)

son. This one _____ to me. It can also be a mother's way

(6)

of _____ her hubby. "When they're giving their name to a

(7)

child, they're giving an _____, or approval," says behavioral

(8)

psychologist Matt Wallaert. He's named after his dad and says he's closer to

his _____ than his brother is. "It does provide the early chance

(9)

for this _____ bonding."

(10)

But the _____(11) Junior—not to mention IIIs, IVs, and Vs—is something of a dying breed, says Cleveland Evans, a psychology _____(12) at Bellevue University in Nebraska who _____(13) in omnastics, or the study of names. "The percentage of juniors has been going _____(14) in American culture in general over the last 40 years at least," says Evans, adding that in the Hispanic community, it remains a _____(15) naming trend. "I think that it's become more of a _____(16) for people to have every child have an _____(17) name," Evans continues. "There's more emphasis on individualism, there's less _____(18) to carry on family names than there _____(19) to be, and there's much more worry about the _____(20) of what happens when you have two people of the same name in the same family."

The Birth-Order Myth

by Alfie Kohn

Health

Prereading Preparation

1 How many brothers and sisters do you have? Are you the youngest? Are you the oldest?

2 Many people believe that birth order affects an individual's personality or intelligence. What do you think about this idea?

3 **a.** Write some general statements describing your classmates' personalities.

b. Make a chart on the board of how many people in the class are *only children, firstborn, secondborn, thirdborn*, etc.

c. Form groups according to birth order; in other words, all the *only children* will form one group, all the *firstborns* will form another group, etc. In your groups, describe your personalities. Make a list of the personality characteristics that are common to all of you.

d. Write the information for each group on the board. Compare all the groups' responses. Discuss how these responses correspond to the descriptions of the other students in the class.

The Birth-Order Myth

1 "No wonder he's so charming and funny—he's the baby of the family!" "She works hard trying to please the boss. I bet she's a firstborn." "Anyone that selfish has to be an only child."

It's long been part of *folk wisdom* that birth order strongly affects personality, **5** intelligence, and achievement. However, most of the research claiming that firstborns are radically different from other children has been discredited, and it now seems that any effects of birth order on intelligence or personality will likely be washed out by all the other influences in a person's life. In fact, the belief in the permanent impact of birth order, according to Toni Falbo, a social **10** psychologist at the University of Texas at Austin, "comes from the psychological theory that your personality is fixed by the time you're six. That assumption simply is incorrect."

The better, later, and larger studies are less likely to find birth order a useful predictor of anything. When two Swiss social scientists, Cecile Ernst and Jules **15** Angst, reviewed 1,500 studies a few years ago, they concluded that "birth-order differences in personality . . . are nonexistent in our sample. In particular, there is no evidence for a 'firstborn personality.'"

Putting Birth Order in Context

Of the early studies that seemed to show birth order mattered, most failed to recognize how other factors could confuse the issue. Take family size: Plenty **20** of surveys showed that eldest children were overrepresented among high achievers. However, that really says less about being a firstborn than about not having many siblings, or any at all. After all, any group of firstborns is going to include a disproportionate number of children from small families, since every family has a firstborn but fewer have a fourthborn. Most experts now **25** believe that position in the family means little when taken out of the context of *everything* going on in a particular household—whether sibling rivalry is promoted or discouraged, for instance.

Parents who believe that firstborns are more capable or deserving may treat them differently, thus setting up a self-fulfilling prophecy.

Old Theories Die Hard

30   Consider the question of whether birth order affects achievement or intelligence. Many experts today suggest that birth order plays no role at all. When Judith Blake, a demographer at the University of California, Los Angeles, looked at birth patterns before 1938 and compared them to SAT[1] scores for that group of children, she found no connection. On the other hand, the *number* of siblings

35   does matter. "Small families are, on average, much more supportive of the kind of verbal ability that helps people succeed in school," Blake says. The reason, she believes, is that parental attention is diluted in larger families.

        As for effects on personality, results are mixed. Research suggests that you're somewhat more likely to be outgoing, well-adjusted and independent

40   if you grew up with few or no siblings. Two recent studies, however, found no differences on the basis of size alone. The only certainty is that there don't seem to be any *disadvantages* to growing up in a small family—including being an only child. After reviewing 141 studies, Falbo and a colleague found that being raised with or without siblings doesn't affect personality in predictable ways. Where

45   small differences were found—such as in achievement motivation—they favored the only children.

Do Kids Need More Space?

        If position doesn't control destiny and family size has only a minor impact, what about spacing between children? Although little research has been conducted, some psychologists believe there are more advantages to having kids

50   far apart rather than close together. Some specialists caution that siblings close in age may be treated as a single unit.

        This is eyebrow-raising news, given that parents are sometimes advised not to wait too long before having a second child. However, different studies have led to different conclusions. One found that a firstborn was more likely to have

55   high self-esteem if his or her sibling was *less* than two years younger. Another indicated that spacing had no impact on social competence, and others note positive effects for boys but not for girls.

        As with birth order, cautions about jumping to conclusions may be ignored by the general public. As Blake says: "You're never going to completely put to rest

60   what people think is fun to believe."

[1]The Scholastic Aptitude Test; the scores on this test are used to determine high school students' ability to do college work.

Fact-Finding Exercise

Read the passage again. Then read the following statements. Scan the article quickly to see if they are True (T) or False (F). If a statement is false, rewrite it so that it is true.

1   _____ T _____ F   The firstborn child in the family is different from the other children in the family.

_____

2   _____ T _____ F   Studies will probably find that birth order affects personality.

_____

3   _____ T _____ F   The number of children in a family affects personality more than birth order does.

_____

4 _____ T _____ F   Growing up in a small family has many disadvantages.

_____

5 _____ T _____ F   Many experts believe that birth order does not affect intelligence.

_____

6 _____ T _____ F   Some people believe it is better for a family to have children far apart rather than close in age.

_____

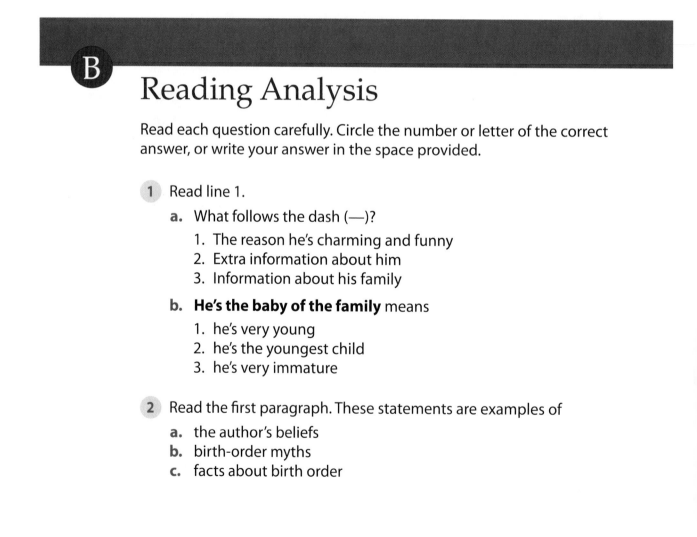

B Reading Analysis

Read each question carefully. Circle the number or letter of the correct answer, or write your answer in the space provided.

1 Read line 1.

   a. What follows the dash (—)?

     1. The reason he's charming and funny
     2. Extra information about him
     3. Information about his family

   b. He's the baby of the family means

     1. he's very young
     2. he's the youngest child
     3. he's very immature

2 Read the first paragraph. These statements are examples of

   a. the author's beliefs
   b. birth-order myths
   c. facts about birth order

3 In line 6, **discredited** means

    a. proved correct

    b. misunderstood

    c. found to be wrong

4 Read lines 5–12.

    a. This statement means that, as a result of other influences, the effects of birth order

        1. will disappear

        2. will become clear

        3. will combine

    b. What information follows **in fact?**

        1. True information about birth order

        2. Information about Toni Falbo

        3. Information to support the previous idea

    c. What word in these sentences is a synonym for **assumption?**

        1. Influence

        2. Belief

        3. Fact

5 Read lines 14–17.

    a. What do the dots between **personality** and **are** indicate?

        1. Some words have been deleted.

        2. Both Ernst and Angst are speaking at the same time.

        3. It is a quotation.

    b. What does **in particular** mean?

        1. Part of

        2. Specifically

        3. In addition

6 In line 19, what does **take** mean?

_____

7 Read lines 24–27.

    a. Why is **_everything_** in italics?

    _____

    b. The author means that

        1. sibling rivalry is important

        2. position in the family is important

        3. all things that are going on are important

c. What is the purpose of the dash (—) after **household?**
1. To add extra information
2. To give an example
3. To give a definition

d. How do you know this is the purpose of the dash?

_____

8 Read lines 31–35.

a. What is the **SAT?**

_____

b. How do you know?

_____

c. This type of information is called
1. an abbreviation
2. a footnote
3. an asterisk

d. **On the other hand** indicates
1. more information
2. an example
3. an opposing idea

e. Why is *number* in italics?

_____

9 Read line 38. **Results are mixed** means
a. different people got different results
b. everyone got the same results
c. different people were confused about their results

10 Read lines 47–48. **Spacing between children** means
a. how far apart children stand
b. how far apart children are in age
c. how far apart children are from their parents

11 Read lines 52–53. **Eyebrow-raising news** is
a. wonderful
b. terrible
c. surprising

Information Organization

Read the article again. Underline what you think are the main ideas. Then scan the article and complete the following outline, using the sentences that you have underlined to help you. You will use this outline later to answer specific questions about the article.

I. The Myth and the Reality about Birth Order

    A. The Myth: _____

    B. The Reality: _____

II. _____

    A. The findings of Cecile Ernst and Jules Angst

        1. Birth-order differences in personality are nonexistent

        2. _____

    B. _____

        1. Birth order does not affect intelligence; she looked at birth patterns before 1938 and compared them to SAT scores for that group of children, and she found no connection

III. _____

    A. _____

        1. It does affect intelligence; small families tend to be more supportive of the kind of verbal ability that helps people succeed in school

    B. _____

        1. Parents who believe that firstborns are more capable or deserving may treat them differently, thus setting up a self-fulfilling prophecy

    C. _____

        1. Some psychologists believe there are more advantages to having kids far apart

        2. One study found that a firstborn was more likely to have high self-esteem if his or her sibling was *less* than two years younger

IV. _____

    A. You're more likely to be outgoing, well-adjusted, and independent if you grew up with few or no siblings

    B. _____

    C. One study indicated that spacing had no impact on social competence

D Information Organization Quiz and Summary

Read each question carefully. Use your notes to answer the questions. Do not refer back to the text. When you are finished, write a brief summary of the article.

1 a. What do many people believe about birth order?

_____

_____

b. What is the truth about birth order?

_____

_____

2 What were the research results about birth order?

_____

_____

3 What are three family factors that may have more effect on personality and intelligence than birth order? Explain each one.

a. _____

b. _____

c. _____

4 Were all the results of research about family size and birth order the same?

_____

_____

Summary

_____

_____

_____

_____

_____

_____

E Dictionary Skills

Read the dictionary entry for each word. Then look at how the word is used in the sentence. Write the number of the correct definition and the synonym or meaning in the space provided. **Be sure to use the correct forms of the verbs and nouns.**

1 **radical** *adj.* **1** having very strong nontraditional beliefs, ideas: *Radical students protested the President's visit to their college campus.* **2** very unusual, different from what is normal: *We noticed a radical difference in our son's behavior after he finished college and got a job.*

People no longer believe that there is a (   ) _____ difference between firstborn children and other children.

2 **claim** *v.* [T] **1** to state s.t. as being true, esp. when there is some doubt, maintain: *She claims that she has a college degree.* **2** to take possession of as a right: *After the airplane landed, I claimed my luggage.* See: claim check.

People no longer (   ) _____ that there is a radical difference between firstborn children and other children.

3 **environment** *n.* **1** [C; U] the air, land, water, and surroundings that people, plants, and animals live in: *The environment in big cities is usually polluted.* **2** [C] a set of social conditions that affect people, an atmosphere: *That child is growing up in a bad environment.* *-adj.* **environmental;** *-adv.* **environmentally.**

The assumption that heredity and our (   ) _____ set our personality by the time we're six is incorrect.

4 **promote** *v.* [T] **-moted, -moting, -motes** **1** to advance in rank, give s.o. a better job: *Her boss promoted her to supervisor in accounting.* **2** to make known to the public, advertise goods and services: *The marketing department promoted our new product in television commercials.* **3** to support, propose, esp. for the public good: *The mayor promoted the idea of building a new sports stadium in the city.* *-adj.* **promotable.**

Some parents (   ) _____ sibling rivalry among their children.

[C]—Countable (noun); [U]—Uncountable (noun); s.o.—someone, s.t.—something; *(syn.)*—synonym; *n.*—noun; *v.*—verb; I—Intransitive; T—Transitive

F Word Forms

PART 1

In English, verbs can change to nouns in several ways. Some verbs become nouns by adding the suffix -*ment,* for example, *improve (v.), improvement (n.).*

Complete each sentence with the correct form of the words on the left. **Use the correct tense of the verbs, in either the affirmative or the negative form. Use the singular or plural form of the nouns.**

encourage *(v.)*

encouragement *(n.)*

1 When Kevin gets married and has children, he _____ them to work hard. Kevin believes that strong parental _____ makes children successful.

achieve *(v.)*

achievement *(n.)*

2 Most big _____ result from hard work. We may not always be successful, but surely we _____ anything if we don't try.

improve *(v.)*

improvement *(n.)*

3 The mayor plans to make significant _____ to all the city parks. First, the mayor _____ the tennis courts and baseball fields. Then she will put in new park benches.

state *(v.)*

statement *(n.)*

4 This morning, the president _____ that he would not run for reelection. He made this surprising _____ at a news conference in Washington, D.C.

treat (v.)

treatment (n.)

5 Doctors usually _____ infections with antibiotics. A severe infection may require several _____ over a long period of time.

In English, some adjectives become nouns by deleting a final -t and adding -ce, for example, *important (adj.), importance (n.).*

Complete each sentence with the correct form of the words on the left.

competent (adj.)

competence (n.)

1 Winifred is an extremely _____ businesswoman. After working at a firm for only a few years, she developed enough _____ to start her own business, which has become very successful.

intelligent (adj.)

intelligence (n.)

2 It is impossible to measure _____ on a test because people have different kinds of aptitudes. Besides, even a very _____ person can become nervous and do poorly on a test.

permanent (adj.)

permanence (n.)

3 Peter has never had a really _____ home. His parents have always moved from one city to another every few years, so the idea of _____ is something very strange to him.

significant (adj.)

significance (n.)

4 There has been a _____ decrease in the population of this city in the last 10 years. The _____ of this population decline in schools is that there tend to be fewer students in each class.

different *(adj.)*

difference *(n.)*

5 I can't taste any _____ between regular coffee and decaffeinated coffee. However, I drink them at _____ times of the day. For instance, I drink regular coffee in the morning, but I drink decaffeinated coffee in the evening.

Word Partnership	Use *intelligence* with:
adj.	**human** intelligence, **secret** intelligence
v.	intelligence **agent**, intelligence **expert**, **military** intelligence

Word Partnership	Use *difference* with:
adj.	**big/major** difference
v.	**know the** difference, **notice a** difference, **tell the** difference, **settle a** difference, **pay the** difference, **make a** difference
n.	difference **in age**, difference **in price**

Critical Thinking Strategies

Read each question carefully, and write a response. Remember that there is no one correct answer. Your response depends on what **you** think.

1 The author writes, "Parents who believe that firstborns are more capable or deserving may treat them differently, thus setting up a self-fulfilling prophecy." The self-fulfilling prophecy is that children live up to their parents' expectations. How do you think parents influence their children by treating them differently?

_____

_____

_____

_____

2 According to the article, the number of siblings a person has affects his or her personality. As Judith Blake says, "Small families are, on average, much more supportive of the kind of verbal ability that helps people succeed in school." The reason, she believes, is that parental attention is diluted in larger families. Why do you think parental attention might be diluted in larger families? Do you agree with this theory? Explain your answer.

_____

_____

_____

_____

3 One study found that a firstborn was more likely to have high self-esteem if his or her sibling was *less* than two years younger. Another indicated that spacing had no impact on social competence, and others note positive effects for boys but not for girls. What conclusion can you make about these different studies?

_____

_____

_____

_____

4 The studies that the author refers to in this article came up with very different results. How do you think we might explain these different findings?

_____

_____

_____

_____

5 Read the last paragraph of the article. What does Judith Blake mean? Why may people ignore the findings about the birth-order myth?

_____

_____

_____

_____

6 What do you think the author's opinion about birth order is? Why do you think so?

_____

_____

_____

_____

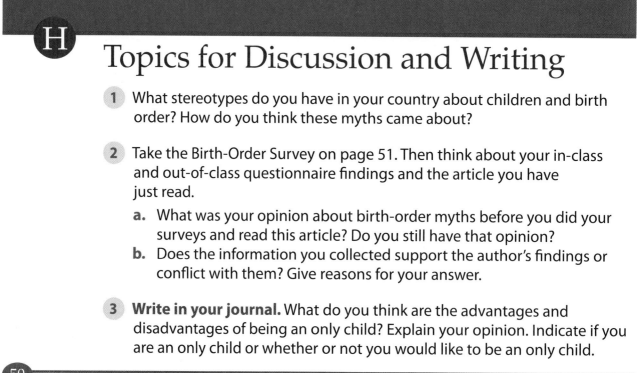

H Topics for Discussion and Writing

1 What stereotypes do you have in your country about children and birth order? How do you think these myths came about?

2 Take the Birth-Order Survey on page 51. Then think about your in-class and out-of-class questionnaire findings and the article you have just read.

   a. What was your opinion about birth-order myths before you did your surveys and read this article? Do you still have that opinion?

   b. Does the information you collected support the author's findings or conflict with them? Give reasons for your answer.

3 **Write in your journal.** What do you think are the advantages and disadvantages of being an only child? Explain your opinion. Indicate if you are an only child or whether or not you would like to be an only child.

Follow-Up Activity

1   **a.** Refer to the Birth Order Survey below. As a class, add more pairs of adjectives to complete the survey. Be sure that adjectives in some of the pairs describe yourself as well.

     b. After you have finished the questionnaire, go outside your class alone or in pairs. Survey two or three people. Then bring back your data and combine it with the other students' information. How do your results compare with the results you obtained in your class? Do you think the idea of birth-order characteristics is convincing, or is it a myth?

Birth-Order Survey

The purpose of this questionnaire is to collect data regarding birth order. Please answer the following questions.

1. Do you have siblings? How many? _____

2. What is your order of birth? That is, are you an *only child, firstborn, secondborn, thirdborn*? Are you also the youngest child?

   _____

3. Choose one word from each pair of adjectives below that best describes your personality.

   1. anxious / confident
   2. patient / impatient
   3. boring / interesting
   4. talkative / quiet
   5. understanding / insensitive
   6. diligent / lazy
   7. friendly / disagreeable
   8. competitive / cooperative
   9. considerate / thoughtless
   10. creative / unimaginative
   11. curious / indifferent
   12. dependent / independent
   13. mature / immature
   14. funny / serious
   15. _____
   16. _____
   17. _____
   18. _____
   19. _____
   20. _____
   21. _____
   22. _____
   23. _____
   24. _____

Cloze Quiz

Complete the passage with words from the list. Use each word only once.

affects	different	influences	research
assumption	discredited	intelligence	scientists
birth	effects	permanent	studies
concluded	evidence	personality	theory
differences	however	predictor	time

It's long been part of *folk wisdom* that birth order strongly

_____ personality, _____ and achievement.
(1)   (2)

_____ , most of the _____ claiming that
(3)   (4)

firstborns are radically _____ from other children has been
(5)

_____ , and it now seems that any _____ of
(6)   (7)

birth order on intelligence or _____ will likely be washed
(8)

out by all the other _____ in a person's life. In fact, the belief
(9)

in the _____ impact of _____ order, according
(10)   (11)

to Toni Falbo, "comes from the psychological _____ that
(12)

your personality is fixed by the _____ you're six. That
(13)

_____ simply is incorrect."
(14)

The better, later, and larger _____ are less likely to find
(15)

birth order a useful _____ of anything. When two Swiss
(16)

social _____ , Cecile Ernst and Jules Angst, reviewed 1,500
(17)

studies a few years ago, they _____ that "birth-order
(18)

_____ in personality . . . are nonexistent in our sample. In
(19)

particular, there is no _____ for a 'firstborn personality.'"
(20)

Crossword Puzzle

Read the clues on the next page. Write the answers in the correct spaces in the puzzle.

Crossword Puzzle Clues

3. Mark's _____, Mark Allen, Jr., is 15 years old.
9. I _____ that woman. She works in my office.
10. We _____ our friendship. It is very important to us.
11. Feelings, such as happiness, anger, or joy
13. One, two, three, _____
14. Competition between people
15. I have; he _____
19. My father and I are very _____. We have a tight bond.
20. Very unhappy
22. Brothers and sisters
24. The opposite of **down**
25. We always _____ our children to do well in school.
28. Surroundings; everything around you

1. Emphasize
2. The opposite of **no**
4. A supposition or belief
5. You look like your mother. You _____ her.
6. My sister and I have a tight _____. We are very close.
7. The mayor was _____ when people found out he had lied about his past.
8. _____ are people who do studies.
12. **Am, is,** _____.
16. Our children are our _____.
17. Concern
18. When two people in a family have the same name, it sometimes causes _____.
19. I _____ do that. I know how.
21. Mostly
23. My father's name is Thomas Johnson. I am Thomas Johnson, _____.
26. The opposite of **on**
27. The past of **give**

Discussion

1. The articles in Unit 1 all relate to what influences our satisfaction in our lives. Discuss what factors in our lives we can control or change, e.g. happiness and names, and those we cannot, e.g. birth order. Which factors do you think are the most important towards achieving satisfaction? Why? Explain your reasons.

2. Can our names affect our place in society? Can our names affect our happiness? Discuss your answers with your class.

3. How does birth order affect our happiness? Do you think that children from large families are happier than children from small families? Why or why not? Give some examples from your own experience.

Health and Well-Being

4 CHAPTER

Laughter Is the Best Medicine for Your Heart

by Michelle W. Murray, *University of Maryland Medical Center*

Prereading Preparation

1. What makes you laugh—for example movies, jokes, etc.?

2. Are there some actors or comedians that make you laugh? Who are they?

3. Do you like to laugh? How do you feel after you laugh?

4 Read the title of the article. The title means:

    a. Laughter can make you feel happy.
    b. You need medicine for your heart.
    c. Laughter is good for your health.

Track 04

Laughter Is the Best Medicine for Your Heart

1   Can a laugh every day keep the heart attack away? Maybe so. Laughter, along with an active sense of humor, may help protect you against a heart attack, according to a recent study by cardiologists at the University of Maryland Medical Center in Baltimore. The study, which is the first to indicate

5   that laughter may help prevent heart disease, found that people with heart disease were 40 percent less likely to laugh in a variety of situations compared to people of the same age without heart disease.

    "The old saying that 'laughter is the best medicine,' definitely appears to be true when it comes to protecting your heart," says Michael Miller, M.D., director

10   of the Center for Preventive Cardiology at the University of Maryland Medical Center and associate professor of medicine at the University of Maryland School of Medicine. "We don't know yet why laughing protects the heart, but we know that mental stress is associated with impairment of the endothelium, the protective barrier lining our blood vessels. This can cause a series of

15   inflammatory reactions that lead to fat and cholesterol build-up in the coronary arteries and ultimately to a heart attack."

    In the study, researchers compared the humor responses of 300 people. Half of the participants had either suffered a heart attack or undergone coronary artery bypass surgery. The other 150 did not have heart disease. One questionnaire had

20   a series of multiple-choice answers to find out how much or how little people laughed in certain situations, and the second one used true or false answers to measure anger and hostility. Miller said that the most significant study finding was that "people with heart disease responded less humorously to everyday life situations." They generally laughed less, even in positive situations, and they

25   displayed more anger and hostility.

"The ability to laugh—either naturally or as learned behavior—may have important implications in societies such as the United States where heart disease remains the number one killer," says Miller. "We know that exercising, not smoking, and eating foods low in saturated fat will reduce the risk of heart disease. Perhaps regular, hearty laughter should be added to the list."

Miller says it may be possible to incorporate laughter into our daily activities, just as we do with other heart-healthy activities, such as taking the stairs instead of the elevator. "We could perhaps read something humorous or watch a funny video and try to find ways to take ourselves less seriously," Miller says. "The recommendation for a healthy heart may one day be exercise, eat right, and laugh a few times a day."

Fact-Finding Exercise

Read the passage again. Then read the following statements. Scan the article quickly to see if they are True (T) or False (F). If a statement is false, rewrite it so that it is true.

1 _____ T _____ F Laughter may protect you from heart disease.

_____

2 _____ T _____ F Doctors understand why laughing prevents heart attacks.

_____

3 _____ T _____ F All of the people in the study had heart disease.

_____

4 _____ T _____ F According to the study, people with heart disease had more anger and hostility than people without heart disease.

_____

5 _____ T _____ F Heart disease is the number one killer in the United States.

_____

6 _____ T _____ F Michael Miller was one of the participants in the study.

_____

Reading Analysis

Read each question carefully. Circle the number or letter of the correct answer, or write your answer in the space provided.

1 Read line 1. **Maybe so** means

   a. maybe by laughing every day, you'll never need medicine for your heart

   b. maybe laughing every day will help prevent a heart attack

   c. maybe laughing every day will cause a heart attack

2 In line 3, **cardiologists** are people who study

   a. heart disease

   b. laughter

   c. humor

3 Read lines 4–7. This sentence means that people with heart disease

   a. laugh as much as 40 percent of the time in a variety of situations

   b. laugh 40 percent more often in the same situations than people without heart disease

   c. do not laugh as much in the same situations as people without heart disease do

4 Read lines 8–12. **When it comes to** means

   a. with regard to

   b. the time of

   c. the arrival of

5 Read lines 12–14.

   a. **Impairment** means

      1. damage

      2. strengthening

      3. identification

   b. What is the **endothelium?**

_____

_____

c. How do you know?

_____

_____

6 Read lines 17–19.

a. **Coronary** refers to
  1. fat
  2. cholesterol
  3. the heart

b. Who are the **participants?**
  1. The people in the study
  2. The people who had heart attacks
  3. The researchers

c. How many people in the study had heart disease?

_____

d. According to the results of the study, who laughed less?
  1. People without heart disease
  2. People with heart disease
  3. People who were angry

7 Read lines 26–28. The information between the dashes (—)
  a. provides more information about the kinds of laughter
  b. explains how laughter affects heart disease
  c. describes the meaning of laughter in some societies

8 Read lines 34–36. According to these sentences, how many factors may help reduce the risk of heart disease?
  a. 2
  b. 3
  c. 4

Information Organization

Read the article again. Underline what you think are the main ideas. Then scan the article. Fill in the following chart about the article, using the sentences that you have underlined to help you. You will use this chart later to answer specific questions about the article.

Laughter Is the Best Medicine for Your Heart	
Who performed the study?	
Why did they do the study?	
Where did they do the study?	
Whom did they study?	
How did they study them?	
What were the results of the study?	
What are the recommendations?	

Information Organization
Quiz and Summary

Read each question carefully. Use your notes and the chart on the previous page to answer the questions. Do not refer back to the text. When you are finished, write a brief summary of the article.

1 What do doctors believe about laughter?

_____

_____

2 Where was the research done?

_____

_____

3 How many people did the researchers study? Did all of them have heart disease?

_____

_____

4 Describe the two questionnaires that the researchers used. How were they different?

_____

_____

5 What did the researchers learn from the study?

_____

_____

6 How can we improve our health with laughter?

_____

_____

Summary

_____

_____

_____

_____

_____

_____

E Dictionary Skills

Read the dictionary entry for each word. Then look at how the word is used in the sentence. Write the number of the correct definition and the synonym or meaning in the space provided. **Be sure to use the correct form of the verbs and nouns.**

1. > **buildup** *n.* **1** growth, (syn.) an increase: *There was a heavy buildup of dust in our house when we came back from vacation.* **2** improving an image or reputation through advertising, (syn.) a publicity campaign: *The British rock stars got a big buildup before their tour.*

   This can cause a series of inflammatory reactions that lead to fat and

   cholesterol (   ) _____ in the coronary arteries and

   ultimately to a heart attack.

2. > **implication** *n.* **1** [U] an indication of participation or involvement of others, esp. in a crime: *The woman's implication of her brother sent him to jail.* **2** [C] an indirect suggestion: *John made implications that Mr. Lu had faked his wife's signature.*

   The ability to laugh—either naturally or as learned behavior—may have

   important (   ) _____ in societies such as the U.S.

   where heart disease remains the number one killer.

3   **incorporate**   *v.* [T] **-rated, -rating, -rates** **1** to include, contain: *The spending agreement incorporates ideas from both Democrats and Republicans.* **2** to form a corporation: *Many people incorporate their businesses to avoid certain taxes.* *-adj.* **incorporated;** *-n.* [U] **incorporation.**

Miller says it may be possible to (   ) _____ laughter

into our daily activities.

Word Forms

PART 1

In English, some adjectives become nouns by adding the suffix *-ity*, for example, *equal (adj.), equality (n.).*

Complete each sentence with the correct form of the words on the left. **Use the singular or plural form of the nouns.**

able *(adj.)*   **1**   Jackie has the _____ to speak several

ability *(n.)*   different languages. As a result, she is _____

                   to travel to many countries very easily.

active *(adj.)*   **2**   Beth enjoys many _____ , such as swimming,

activity *(n.)*   biking, and hiking. It's easy to see that she is a very

                   _____ person!

hostile *(adj.)*   **3**   The strange dogs were _____ to Jack when

hostility *(n.)*   he entered their cage. However, their _____

                   quickly stopped when Jack began to feed them.

possible *(adj.)*

possibility *(n.)*

4 There is a _____ that it may rain tomorrow, so I'll carry an umbrella to school in case of a _____ downpour.

responsible *(adj.)*

responsibility *(n.)*

5 Having children is a huge _____. Parents are _____ for their children's safety, health, education, and socialization.

PART 2

In English, some adjectives become nouns by deleting the final *-t* and adding *-ce*, for example, *independent (adj.), independence (n.).*
   Complete each sentence with a correct form of the words on the left.

excellent *(adj.)*

excellence *(n.)*

1 The food at the new Italian restaurant is _____. Because of the _____ of its food, it's difficult to find a table there.

negligent *(adj.)*

negligence *(n.)*

2 My uncle was very _____ about his health. Unfortunately, his _____ caused him to become very sick for a long time.

dependent *(adj.)*

dependence *(n.)*

3 Children are always _____ on their parents. However, their _____ decreases as they get older.

important *(adj.)*

importance *(n.)*

4 My doctor discussed the _____ of eating a healthy breakfast every morning. This is very _____ advice.

significant *(adj.)*

significance *(n.)*

5 After Tom stopped eating fast food, he noticed a _____ change in his weight. The _____ of eating food that is low in fat became very clear to him.

Word Partnership	Use *importance* with:
adj.	**critical** importance, **enormous** importance, **growing/increasing** importance, **utmost** importance
v.	**place less/more** importance **on** *something*, **recognize the** importance, **understand the** importance
n.	**self-**importance, **sense of** importance

Word Partnership	Use *significance* with:
adj.	**cultural** significance, **great** significance, **historic** significance, **political** significance, **religious** significance
v.	**downplay the** significance **of** *something*, **explain the** significance **of** *something*, **understand the** significance **of** *something*

Critical Thinking Strategies

Read each question carefully, and write a response. Remember that there is no one correct answer. Your response depends on what **you** think.

1 Many doctors believe that mental stress may cause heart disease. Why do you think laughter helps prevent heart disease?

_____

_____

_____

2 In a study, cardiologists found that people with heart disease "generally laughed less, even in positive situations, and they displayed more anger and hostility" than did people without heart disease.

    a. Why do you think they laughed less?

_____

_____

_____

_____

    b. Why do you think they displayed more anger and hostility?

_____

_____

_____

_____

3 Is humor culturally determined? In other words, does what we think of as funny depend on the culture we grew up in? Do people from the same culture think that the same things are funny?

_____

_____

_____

_____

H Topics for Discussion and Writing

1 Do you think that the ability to laugh is a natural behavior or a learned behavior? In other words, is the ability to laugh innate, like the ability to sing, or is it something we can learn to do? Explain your answer.

2 Describe a funny movie that you have seen. What was the name of the movie? What was funny about the movie?

3 **Write in your journal.** Describe an incident or a story that you think is humorous—something that made you laugh.

Follow-Up Activities

1 Read the article and do the activities on page 72.

Laughter Really Is Best Medicine

Class combining deep breathing, yoga shows benefits

by Jennifer L. Boen

The News-Sentinel

1   It's often said, "Attitude is everything," but most people have experienced the reality that when feeling down or lacking self-confidence, taking action transforms attitude. Such is the premise of Laughter Yoga, a technique gaining popularity across the United States. Laughter Yoga is based on the philosophy
5   of "acting happiness." Even when you don't feel like laughing, the physical act of doing so increases feel-good chemicals in the body, says Fort Wayne certified Laughter Yoga leader Lee Wilcher. "The body cannot differentiate between fake and real laughter, so when you go through the motions of laughter, it produces the same physiological and psychological effects," he said. Humor is a left-brain,
10   analytical process, but laughing for no reason engages the right or creative side of the brain.

Laughter Yoga, which combines deep breathing, stretching, and laughter exercises, was founded by Madan Kataria in 1995 after he did extensive research on the physical and emotional benefits of laughing. He encourages leaders who
15   run Laughter Yoga groups to make them free and open to anyone. It can be practiced alone, but doing it within a group has added benefits.

Several studies back up the premise that laughing has beneficial results, physiologically and emotionally. One study of information technology workers in India showed the group that participated in Laughter Yoga sessions over
20   18 days had significantly lowered heart rates and blood pressure readings, plus a 17-percent increase in positive emotions and a 27-percent decrease in negative emotions compared to the control group.

a. According to the article, even when we don't feel like it, laughing has physical and psychological benefits. On your own, test out this statement. Do this by yourself if you do not feel comfortable. Pick a time when you do not feel like laughing. Laugh anyway, out loud, for several minutes. Be sure to breathe deeply and laugh out loud for a few minutes. Then examine how you feel. Write down how you felt before you laughed, and how you felt after you laughed. Bring your report to class, and share it with your classmates. How many students felt the same after laughing? How many students felt better?

b. According to the article, Laughter Yoga can be practiced alone, but doing it within a group has added benefits. As a class, perform this experiment. All the students will write down how they feel at the moment. Then the entire class will begin laughing, out loud, for several minutes. Then all the students will write down how they feel. How many students feel the same? How many students feel better?

2 Take a survey among the class. Does laughing alone make you feel better? Does laughing in a group make you feel better?

J Cloze Quiz

Complete the passage with words from the list. Use each word only once.

anger	disease	implications	protecting
attack	heart	laughter	significant
build-up	hostility	learned	situations
cardiologists	humor	medicine	variety
coronary	impairment	percent	without

Can a laugh every day keep the heart _____ away?
(1)

Maybe so. Laughter, along with an active sense of _____ ,
(2)

may help protect you against a heart attack, according to a recent study

by _____ at the University of Maryland Medical Center in
(3)

Baltimore. The study, which is the first to indicate that _____ (4) may help prevent heart _____ (5), found that people with heart disease were 40 _____ (6) less likely to laugh in a _____ (7) of situations compared to people of the same age _____ (8) heart disease.

"The old saying that 'laughter is the best _____ (9),' definitely appears to be true when it comes to _____ (10) your heart," says Michael Miller, M.D. "We don't know yet why laughing protects the _____ (11), but we know that mental stress is associated with _____ (12) of the endothelium, the protective barrier lining our blood vessels. This can cause a series of inflammatory reactions that lead to fat and cholesterol _____ (13) in the coronary arteries and ultimately to a heart attack."

In the study, researchers compared the humor responses of 300 people. Half of the participants had either suffered a heart attack or undergone _____ (14) artery bypass surgery. The other 150 did not have heart disease. One questionnaire had a series of multiple-choice answers to find out how much or how little people laughed in certain _____ (15), and the second one used true or false answers to measure anger and _____ (16). Miller said that the most _____ (17) study finding was that "people with heart disease responded less humorously to everyday life situations." They generally laughed less, even in positive situations, and they displayed more _____ (18) and hostility.

"The ability to laugh—either naturally or as _____ (19) behavior— may have important _____ (20) in societies such as the U.S. where heart disease remains the number one killer," says Miller. "We know that exercising, not smoking, and eating foods low in saturated fat will reduce the risk of heart disease. Perhaps regular, hearty laughter should be added to the list."

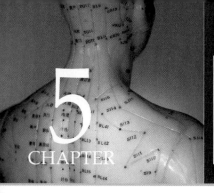
Acupuncture: The New Old Medicine

Edited by William G. Flanagan, *Forbes*

Prereading Preparation

1. What do you know about **acupuncture?** How is it done? Is it a new kind of medicine?

2. Why do people get acupuncture treatments?

3. Have you ever had acupuncture treatments, or do you know someone who has? Describe the experience and the reason for the treatment.

4. Acupuncture is a traditional form of medicine. Do you know of some other traditional kinds of medicine? Are these treatments different from more "modern" medical treatments? How?

5. Read the title of this chapter. Why is acupuncture called the "new old medicine"?

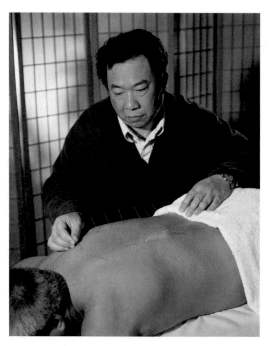

Acupuncture: The New Old Medicine

1   The thin, extremely sharp needles didn't hurt at all going in. Dr. Gong pricked them into my left arm, around the elbow that had been bothering me. Other needles were slipped into my left wrist and, strangely, my *right* arm, and then into both my closed eyelids.

5   There wasn't any discomfort, just a mild warming sensation, when the electrodes were connected to the needles in my left arm, and my muscles began to twitch involuntarily. However, I did begin to wonder what had driven me here, to the office of Dr. James Gong, a floor up from Mott Street in New York's Chinatown.

10   Then I remembered—the excruciating pain in that left elbow. Several trips to a Fifth Avenue neurologist and two expensive, uncomfortable medical tests had failed to produce even a diagnosis. "Maybe you lean on your left arm too much," the neurologist concluded, suggesting I see a bone doctor.

    During the hours spent waiting in vain to see an orthopedist, I decided to take
15   another tack and try acupuncture. A Chinese-American friend recommended Dr. Gong. I took the subway to Canal Street and walked past the open-air fish stalls, the incense shops, the Asia Bank branch, and restaurants with cooked ducks hanging in their windows. Reaching Dr. Gong's second-floor office, marked with a hand painted sign, I felt I could have been in old Hong Kong.

20   Dr. Gong speaks English, but not often. Most of my questions to him were greeted with a friendly laugh, but I managed to let him know where my arm hurt. He hustled me into a room, had me lie down on a cot, and went to work. In the next room, I learned, a woman dancer was also getting a treatment. As I lay there a while, becoming oblivious to the needles and the muscle spasms and
25   the electric current shooting through my arm, I drifted into a dreamlike state and fantasized about what she looked like.

    Not every acupuncturist offers such fantasy trips to China and beyond along with the price of treatment, of course. Acupuncturists today are as likely to be found on Park Avenue as on Mott Street, and they are as likely to be Caucasian
30   as Asian. In all there are an estimated 10,000 acupuncturists in the country, 6,500 of whom are certified one way or another. Nowadays, a lot of M.D.s have learned acupuncture techniques; so have a number of dentists. Reason? Patient demand. Few, though, can adequately explain how acupuncture works.

Acupuncturists may say that the body has more than 800 acupuncture points. A life force called *qi* (pronounced CHEE) circulates through the body. Points on the skin are energetically connected to specific organs, body structures and systems. Acupuncture points are stimulated to balance the circulation of qi. It's all very confusing.

The truth is, though acupuncture is at least 2,200 years old, "nobody really knows what's happening," says Paul Zmiewski, a Ph.D. in Chinese studies who practices acupuncture in Philadelphia.

Millions of Americans now seek out the services of acupuncturists, usually because conventional medicine failed to cure their ills. Jack Tymann, 51, president and general manager of Westinghouse Electronic Systems Co., is typical. Tymann was bothered for 15 years with severe lower back pain. His doctor suggested disc surgery, but he decided to try acupuncture instead.

A scientist and an engineer by education, Tymann was highly skeptical at first. "I went in with that symptom, and haven't had any trouble with my back since," he says. He still goes for treatments, four or five times per year—not for back pain, but as a preventive measure. "It's been my primary form of health care for about nine years now," he says.

Harwood Beville, 51, executive vice president of the Rouse Co., started acupuncture nine years ago, for treatment of "what I'll call tennis shoulder." The shoulder had bothered him for two years, and visits to other doctors met with no success. Acupuncture had worked for his wife. After a few treatments, his pain was gone, and there were other noticeable effects. "Immediately, stress didn't seem to be bothering me so much." Like Tymann, he, too, still goes for regular treatments.

Acupuncture is used to treat a variety of ailments—anxiety, depression, back pain, smoking, high blood pressure, stress, arthritis; the list goes on. Acupuncture is even used to help treat drug addiction—with considerable success.

The number of treatments can vary, although one-shot cures are relatively rare. It usually takes four to six sessions to treat a specific ailment. If that doesn't work, you will probably feel at least somewhat better. After five treatments from Dr. Gong, there has been dramatic improvement in my arm, and the pain is a fraction of what it was. I feel less stress, too. I think. The mainly silent Dr. Gong finally even offered a diagnosis for what ailed me. "Pinched nerve," he said.

Fact-Finding Exercise

Read the passage again. Then read the following statements. Scan the article quickly to see if they are True (T) or False (F). If a statement is false, rewrite it so that it is true.

1 _____T _____F   Dr. Gong is a neurologist.

_____

2 _____T _____F   The neurologist was not able to stop the author's pain.

_____

3 _____T _____F   Dr. Gong's office is on Fifth Avenue.

_____

4 _____T _____F   Dr. Gong does not know how to speak English.

_____

5 _____T _____F   It is hard to explain how acupuncture works.

_____

6 _____T _____F   Jack Tymann continues to visit an acupuncturist because his back still hurts.

_____

7 _____T _____F   Most acupuncture treatments take more than one session.

_____

Reading Analysis

Read each question carefully. Circle the number or letter of the correct answer, or write your answer in the space provided.

1 In the first paragraph, what is a synonym for **pricked into?**

_____

2 In lines 7–9, the author writes, "However, I did begin to wonder **what had driven me** here, to the office of Dr. Gong." This means that the author was thinking about

a. how he had gotten there
b. why he had gone there
c. what Dr. Gong does

3 Read lines 10–12: "Several trips to a Fifth Avenue neurologist and two expensive, uncomfortable medical tests had **failed to produce a diagnosis." Failed to produce a diagnosis** means that

a. the author did not pass his medical tests
b. the tests did not relieve his pain
c. the tests did not uncover his physical problem

4 In lines 12–13, the neurologist suggested that the author see a bone doctor. In the next paragraph, what is a synonym for **bone doctor?**

_____

5 Read lines 14–15: "During the hours spent waiting **in vain** to see an orthopedist, I decided to take another tack and try acupuncture." **In vain** means

a. uselessly
b. carefully
c. quietly

6 In line 23, the author writes, "A woman dancer was also getting a treatment." What does **treatment** mean?

_____

7 In line 29, what are **Park Avenue** and **Mott Street?**

   a. Similar places
   b. Different places
   c. Medical places

8 Read lines 30–31. **"In all,** there are an estimated 10,000 acupuncturists in the country." What does **in all** mean?

   a. In total
   b. In fact
   c. In New York

9 Read lines 31–33: **"Nowadays,** a lot of **M.D.s** have learned acupuncture techniques; so have a number of dentists. Reason? Patient demand. **Few,** though, can adequately explain how acupuncture works."

   a. What does **nowadays** refer to?

      1. Only at the present time
      2. From some time in the past up to the present
      3. During the time that the author's story takes place

   b. What are **M.D.s?**

      1. Doctors
      2. Dentists
      3. Acupuncturists

   c. In line 33, who does **few** refer to?

      1. Only patients
      2. Only M.D.s
      3. Dentists and M.D.s
      4. Only dentists

10 Read line 35: "A life force called **qi** (pronounced CHEE) circulates through the body."

   a. What is **qi?**

      _____

   b. How do you know?

      _____

11 Read lines 43–45: "Jack Tymann, 51, president and general manager of Westinghouse Electronic Systems Co., is typical." This sentence means that Jack Tymann is

   a. a common man
   b. a common example
   c. a common acupuncturist

12 Read lines 45–46: "His doctor suggested disc surgery, but he decided to try acupuncture **instead.**"

   a. Jack Tymann had

      1. surgery, but not acupuncture
      2. surgery and acupuncture
      3. acupuncture, but not surgery

   b. Complete the following sentence correctly.

   Jack and Helen wanted to go to the beach, but it was raining. They decided to

      1. go to the movies instead
      2. go for a walk instead
      3. go for a swim instead

13 Read lines 52–53: "Harwood Beville, 51, executive vice president of the Rouse Co., started acupuncture nine years ago, for treatment of 'what I'll call tennis shoulder.'" How old was Harwood Beville when he started acupuncture?

   a. 51
   b. 42
   c. 60

14 Read lines 59–60: "Acupuncture is used to treat a variety of **ailments**— anxiety, depression, back pain, smoking, high blood pressure, stress, arthritis; the list goes on." What are **ailments?**

   a. Treatments
   b. Problems
   c. Illnesses

Information Organization

Read the article again. Underline what you think are the main ideas. Then scan the article and complete the following outline, using the sentences that you have underlined to help you. You will use this outline later to answer specific questions about the article.

I.   The Author's Thoughts about His First Acupuncture Experience

    A. How the treatment felt

        1. _____

        2. _____

    B. Why he had come to Dr. Gong's office

        1. _____

        2. _____

II. A Description of Today's Acupuncturists

    A. _____

    B. _____

    C. _____

III. A Description of Acupuncture

    A. _____

    B. *A life force called qi (pronounced CHEE) circulates through the body*

    C. _____

    D. _____

    E. *Acupuncture is at least 2,200 years old, but nobody really knows how it works*

IV. Who Gets Acupuncture Treatments

    A. Number of people: _____

    B. Examples of people who have acupuncture treatments:

        1. _____

        2. _____

V. Uses of Acupuncture

   A. _____

   B. _____

VI. Effectiveness of Acupuncture

   A. _____

Information Organization
Quiz and Summary

Read each question carefully. Use your notes to answer the questions. Do not refer back to the text. When you are finished, write a brief summary of the article.

1 Why did the author decide to go to an acupuncturist?

_____

_____

_____

2 What is acupuncture? How does it work?

_____

_____

3 **a.** Why did Jack Tymann go to an acupuncturist? What was the result of his treatments?

_____

_____

_____

b. Why did Harwood Beville go to an acupuncturist? What was the result of his treatments?

_____

_____

_____

4 What can acupuncturists treat?

_____

_____

_____

5 How long do acupuncture treatments usually take?

_____

_____

_____

Summary

_____

_____

_____

_____

_____

_____

Dictionary Skills

Read the dictionary entry for each word. Then look at how the word is used in the sentence. Write the number of the correct definition and the synonym or meaning in the space provided. **Be sure to use the correct form of the verbs and nouns.**

1 conclude *v.* -cluded, -cluding, -cludes **1** [I; T] to bring to an end: *The concert concluded with an exciting song.* **2** [T] to form an opinion: *After not getting a salary increase, I concluded that I must find a new job.* **3** **to reach** or **come to a conclusion:** to come to an agreement: *The agreement was concluded and signed in 1945.*

The neurologist (   ) _____ that perhaps I leaned on my left arm too much and suggested that I see a bone doctor.

2 hustle *v.* -tled, -tling, -tles **1** [I; T] to go rapidly, rush: *I hustled over to my friend's place.* **2** [I] to work energetically: *He really hustled to finish the job on time.* **3** [I; T] to do business in a sneaky or overly aggressive way: *He hustled stolen cars for a living.* **4** *infrml.* [I] to sell one's body as a prostitute

Dr. Gong (   ) _____ me into a room, had me lie

down on a cot, and went to work.

3 fail *v.* **1** [I; T] to not succeed: *He failed his test in math.* **2** [I] to not operate when needed: *The brakes failed on his automobile when he tried to stop.* **3** [I] to break: *A wire failed on a bridge and fell over the roadway.* **4** [I] to lose strength and ability: *The old man is failing rapidly and may die soon.*

Millions of Americans go to acupuncturists, usually because conventional

medicine (   ) _____ . It does not cure their ills.

4 dramatic *adj.* **1** related to drama: *He has written dramatic works for the stage.* **2** related to a high emotional point: *a dramatic scene in a play* **3** making a big impression, (*syn.*) striking: *She wore an amazing dress for a dramatic entrance into the theater.* -adv. **dramatically.**

After five treatments from Dr. Gong, there has been

(   ) _____ improvement in my arm.

F Word Forms

In English, adjectives usually become adverbs by adding the suffix *-ly*, for example, *immediate (adj.), immediately (adv.)*.

Complete each sentence with the correct form of the words on the left.

extreme *(adj.)*

extremely *(adv.)*

1 Some people believe that the death penalty is an

_____ form of punishment. Others

believe that murder is an _____ serious

crime, and that murderers deserve capital punishment.

strange *(adj.)*

strangely *(adv.)*

2 Barbara has been acting very _____

lately. I wonder if anything is wrong. Perhaps I should

ask her about her _____ behavior.

involuntary *(adj.)*

involuntarily *(adv.)*

3 Sometimes people jump when they hear thunder.

This is called an _____ reaction. Many

people react _____ when they hear a

loud noise unexpectedly.

adequate *(adj.)*

adequately *(adv.)*

4 This essay is not _____ . It should be at

least 300 words. You cannot express your point of view

_____ in only 100 words.

usual *(adj.)*

usually *(adv.)*

5 Eve _____ , but not always, takes

her vacation in August. This is because her

_____ vacation consists of relaxing on

the beach and swimming in the ocean.

In English, verbs can change to nouns in several ways. Some verbs become nouns by adding the suffix *-ion* or *-tion*, for example, *prevent (v.), prevention (n.)*.

Complete each sentence with the correct form of the words on the left. **Use the correct tense of the verbs, in either the affirmative or the negative form. Use the singular or plural form of the nouns.**

conclude *(v.)*

conclusion *(n.)*

1 Copernicus, a well-known Polish astronomer, _____ that the Earth was round. He reached his revolutionary _____ in the sixteenth century.

recommend *(v.)*

recommendation *(n.)*

2 John _____ that I take advanced calculus this semester, but I didn't listen to him. I should have taken his advice because his _____ have always been sensible.

stimulate *(v.)*

stimulation *(n.)*

3 Babies need constant _____ in order to help their development. If adults _____ babies' interest in the world around them, they will become more alert.

explain *(v.)*

explanation *(n.)*

4 Yesterday, the teacher _____ how electricity is produced because she didn't have time. Tomorrow, when she gives her scientific _____, I will take notes.

decide (v.)

decision (n.)

(5) I _____ yet where to apply to graduate school. I need to make some other important _____ first, such as whether to stay in this country or go back home.

Word Partnership	Use *explanation* with:
adj.	**brief** explanation, **detailed** explanation, **logical** explanation, **only** explanation, **possible** explanation
v.	**give an** explanation, **offer an** explanation, **provide an** explanation

Word Partnership	Use *decision* with:
v.	**arrive at a** decision, **make a** decision, **postpone a** decision, **reach a** decision
adj.	**difficult** decision, **final** decision, **important** decision, **right** decision, **wise** decision, **wrong** decision

Critical Thinking Strategies

Read each question carefully, and write a response. Remember that there is no one correct answer. Your response depends on what **you** think.

1 In the first paragraph of this passage, the author describes his acupuncture treatment. He writes, "Other needles were slipped into my left wrist and, strangely, my *right* arm, and then into both my closed eyelids." Why did he think this was strange?

_____

_____

_____

_____

2　In lines 10–13, the author talks about his experiences with a "Fifth Avenue neurologist." What do you think the author believed about Fifth Avenue doctors before he had acupuncture treatments?

_____

_____

_____

_____

3　In the third paragraph, the author describes his experience with the Fifth Avenue neurologist. In the fourth paragraph, he recounts his trip to Dr. Gong's office. The author gives different impressions about the two doctors and their environments. What are they?

_____

_____

_____

_____

4　According to this article, Harwood Beville went to an acupuncturist because other doctors could not help him and because "acupuncture had worked for his wife." How do you think Mrs. Beville's experience affected Mr. Beville?

_____

_____

_____

_____

5　Read the last two sentences of this article. What is the tone of these statements? In other words, what is the author's opinion about Dr. Gong?

_____

_____

_____

_____

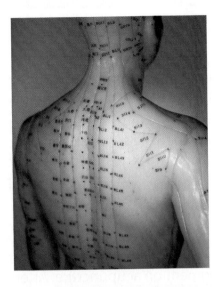

H Topics for Discussion and Writing

1. Many people today are using traditional forms of medicine in place of modern treatments. What do you think are some reasons for this change? Write a composition to explain your answer.

2. a. In a group, make a list of common illnesses. Next to each illness, write the traditional forms of medicine that you know are used to treat these illnesses, both in your country and in other countries. Then write the modern treatments for these illnesses. Compare the two types of treatments for each illness you have chosen. For instance, which treatment is usually less expensive? Which usually takes less time to see positive results? Which seems to be more effective? Which is less extreme, i.e., involves taking medicine or getting therapy, as opposed to having surgery?
   b. For each illness, discuss which type of treatment you would prefer if you had that illness. Explain your reasons to your classmates.
   c. As a class, list on the board all the illnesses that you discussed and the traditional and modern treatments for each. Then take a poll to see how many students prefer the traditional treatments and how many students prefer the modern treatments for these ailments.

3. **Write in your journal.** Select a traditional form of medicine that has been used in your country for a long time. Describe its uses and its effectiveness. Discuss your personal experience with this traditional form or the experience of someone you know. Tell whether you would recommend this form of medicine to others, and why.

Follow-Up Activity

1 **Jigsaw Reading:** You are going to read more information about acupuncture: what it is, how it works, and what it treats.

   a. First, all students read the paragraph titled *Acupuncture*. Discuss it in class to make sure everyone understands it.

   b. Second, work in a group of three or four students. Each group will read different information about acupuncture on the following pages. Group A will read about what acupuncture is; Group B will read about how acupuncture works; Group C will read about what acupuncture treats. If your class is large, then you may have more than one Group A, B, or C; just make sure that at least one group reads about each segment on acupuncture. After reading the paragraph, discuss it to make sure everyone in the group understands their particular segment.

   c. Third, set up different groups so that each group has a student or students who have read each paragraph. In these new groups, tell each other what you have read about acupuncture. In the spaces under your paragraph, take notes about the information the other students give you. Do not look back at your readings. Ask each other questions to make sure that all the students in your group understand all the information about acupuncture.

   d. Finally, work together to answer the questions on page 94. When your group is finished, compare your answers with the other groups' answers.

All Students Read: *Acupuncture*

Acupuncture is a scientific and complete system based on exact laws and principles. It has been used in China for centuries. In fact, classical Chinese acupuncture is one of the oldest forms of medicine known to humankind.

Group A Only: *What Is Acupuncture?*

Acupuncture is a system of medicine used to restore and maintain health, as well as prevent illness. It originated in China over 5,000 years ago and is based on the belief that any illness or symptom is associated with an imbalance in the body's vital life energy. Traditional acupuncture works to restore the natural flow of this energy throughout the body, relieving the underlying cause of the illness and the accompanying symptoms.

Group B's Information:

_____

_____

_____

_____

_____

_____

Group C's Information:

_____

_____

_____

_____

_____

_____

_____

Group B Only: *How Does Acupuncture Work?*

The vital energy, known as *qi* energy, travels in 12 pathways called *meridians.* Each meridian corresponds to a vital organ, such as kidneys, liver, heart, stomach, lungs, etc. Each has a pulse that informs the acupuncturist of the condition of the energy within that meridian. When the acupuncturist inserts very fine needles into points that lie along these meridians, energy is summoned to the places that need it and dispersed from the areas where it is congested. In this way, the natural flow of energy along the pathways is restored and healthy patterns reestablished over time.

Group A's Information:

_____

_____

_____

_____

_____

_____

_____

Group C's Information:

_____

_____

_____

_____

_____

_____

_____

_____

Group C Only: *What Does Acupuncture Treat?*

Acupuncture treats the whole person—the body, the mind, and the spirit—therefore, it can be helpful in the treatment of all conditions. In addition to its widespread use in the relief of pain, acupuncture has been used to treat a wide variety of illnesses both as a primary modality and as an adjunct to traditional western medicine. Acupuncture is useful in treating chronic conditions, e.g., headaches, chronic fatigue, anxiety, and insomnia. It increases energy levels, assists the immune system, and contributes to a person's general well-being.

Group A's Information:

_____

_____

_____

_____

_____

_____

_____

Group B's Information:

_____

_____

_____

_____

_____

_____

_____

_____

Acupuncture Questions

1 What is acupuncture?

_____

_____

2 When did it originate?

_____

_____

3 What belief is acupuncture based on?

_____

_____

4 What is *qi* energy?

_____

_____

5 What is a meridian?

_____

_____

6 How is acupuncture done?

_____

_____

7 How does acupuncture help the patient?

_____

_____

8 How does acupuncture treat the whole person?

_____

_____

9 What illnesses and other problems does acupuncture treat?

_____

_____

Cloze Quiz

Complete the passage with words from the list. Use each word only once.

acupuncture	education	primary	suggested
bothered	instead	services	symptom
conventional	pain	since	treatments
cure	president	skeptical	typical
doctors	preventive	success	visits

Millions of Americans now seek out the _____ of (1) acupuncturists, usually because _____ medicine failed to (2) _____ their ills. Jack Tymann, 51, is _____. (3) (4)

Tymann was _____ for 15 years with severe lower back (5) pain. His doctor _____ disc surgery, but he decided to try (6) acupuncture _____. A scientist and an engineer by (7) _____, Tymann was highly _____ at first. (8) (9) "I went in with that _____ and haven't had any trouble with (10) my back _____," he says. He still goes for _____ (11) (12) four or five times per year—not for back pain, but as a _____ (13) measure. "It's been my _____ form of health care for about nine (14) years now," he says.

Harwood Beville, 51, executive vice _____ of the Rouse Co., (15) started _____ nine years ago. His shoulder had bothered him (16) for two years, and _____ to other _____ met with (17) (18) no _____. After a few treatments, his _____ was (19) (20) gone.

Highs and Lows in Self-Esteem

by Kim Lamb Gregory, *Scripps Howard News Service*

Prereading Preparation

1 Look at the photograph. How do the people in the photo feel about themselves?

2 Work alone. Complete the following chart. How did you feel about yourself at each stage of your life? Was your self-esteem high or low?

Childhood	Adolescence	Young Adulthood	Adulthood

3 Work in a small group. Compare your answers in the chart. Did you all have the same level of self-esteem at the same stages of your lives?

Highs and Lows in Self-Esteem

1   No one in the Gould family of Westlake Village, California, was surprised by a study suggesting a person's age and stage of life may have a bigger impact on self-esteem than we ever realized. A study of about 350,000 people likens a person's self-esteem across the human lifespan to a roller coaster ride,

5   starting with an inflated sense of self-approval in late childhood that plunges in adolescence. Self-esteem rises steadily through adulthood, only to drop to its lowest point ever in old age. "I've gone through pretty much all of those cycles," Fred Gould said. At 60, he's edging toward retirement. Fred's wife, Eileen, 46, is a businesswoman in the throes of mid-adulthood and, according to the

10   study, predisposed to a healthy self-regard. At 21, the Goulds' son, Jeff, has just launched that heady climb into adulthood and a buoyant self-regard after an adolescence fraught with the usual perils of self-doubt and hormonal warfare. His sister, Aly, 17, disagrees with a lot of the study, believing instead that each individual has an intrinsic sense of self-esteem that remains relatively constant.

15   But she does agree that adolescence can give even the most solid sense of self-esteem a sound battering. "As a teenager, I can definitely speak for all of us when I say we bag on ourselves," Aly said.

The Study

    The drop in self-esteem in adolescence was no surprise to Richard Robins, a psychology professor at the University of California at Davis, who spearheaded

20   the study, but "the drop in old age is a little bit more novel," he said. Specifically, Robins was intrigued by the similarities in self-esteem levels between those entering adolescence and old age. "There is an accumulation of losses occurring all at once both in old age and adolescence," he suggested. "There is a critical mass of transition going on."

25   Those answering the survey ranged in age from 9 to 90. They participated in the survey by logging onto a Web site during a period between 1999 and 2000. About three-quarters were Caucasian, the rest a mixture of people of Asian, black, Latino and Middle-Eastern descent. Most were from the United States. The survey simply asked people to agree or strongly disagree—on a five-point

30   scale—with the statement: "I see myself as someone who has high self-esteem."

    Everybody is an individual, Robins stressed, so self-esteem can be affected by a number of things that are biological, social, and situational, but there are certain passages that all of us face—and each passage can have a powerful effect on our sense of self. "With kids, their feelings about themselves are often based

35 on relatively superficial information," Robins explained. "As we get older, we base our self-esteem on actual achievements and feedback from other people."

Overall, the study indicated that women do not fare as well as men in self-esteem—a difference particularly marked in adolescence. "During adolescence, girls' self-esteem dropped about twice as much as boys'," Robins said, perhaps
40 at least partially because of society's heavy emphasis on body image for girls. Add one negative life event to all of this turmoil, and a teenager's delicate self-esteem can crumble.

Emerging into Adulthood

Eileen remembered having fairly high self-esteem from ages 12 to 16. She had been very ill as a child, so the teen years were a time for her to blossom. Then,
45 her mother died when she was 17, and her self-esteem bottomed out. "I was like, 'What do I do? How do I handle this?'" Eileen remembered. Eileen was 22 when she married Fred, an event that coincided with the beginning of her adult years—and an upswing in her self-esteem. Like many adults, Eileen gained her senses of competence and continuity, both of which can contribute to the rise in
50 self-esteem during the adult years, Robins said.

Even if there is divorce or some other form of chaos, there has been a change in our ability to cope, he said. We learn with experience. Fred is aware that his sense of self-esteem may be vulnerable when he retires. "I'm concerned about keeping my awareness level," he said. "Am I going to be aware of the social
55 scene? Of things more global? Am I going to be able to read and keep up with everything?"

Seniors do tend to experience a drop in self-esteem when they get into their 70s, the study says—but not always. This is enigmatic to Robins. "When we look at things like general well-being, the evidence is mixed about what happens in old
60 age," he said.

Some people experience a tremendous loss of self-esteem, whereas others maintain their sense of well-being right through old age. Others are not as lucky. Whereas adolescents lose their sense of childhood omnipotence, seniors experience another kind of loss. Retirement comes at about the same time
65 seniors may begin to lose loved ones, their health, their financial status, or their sense of competence. Suddenly, someone who was so in charge may become withdrawn, sullen, and depressed. Their self-esteem may plummet. Robins hopes the study will make us more aware of the times when our self-esteem can be in jeopardy.

Fact-Finding Exercise

Read the passage again. Then, read the following statements. Scan the article quickly to see if they are True (T) or False (F). If a statement is false, rewrite it so that it is true.

1 _____ T _____ F   A person's self-esteem is high during childhood.

_____

2 _____ T _____ F   A person's self-esteem does not change during adolescence.

_____

3 _____ T _____ F   All people experience their lowest self-esteem during old age.

_____

4 _____ T _____ F   The people in the study were mostly Asian.

_____

5 _____ T _____ F Our self-esteem is affected by several factors.

6 _____ T _____ F Our self-esteem is most delicate when we are adults.

7 _____ T _____ F Older people's self-esteem always drops when they get into their 70s.

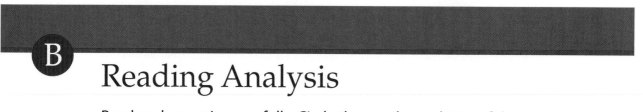

B Reading Analysis

Read each question carefully. Circle the number or letter of the correct answer, or write your answer in the space provided.

1 Read the first paragraph. The author compares the changes in a person's self-esteem over a lifetime to a roller-coaster ride. How does the author think a person's self-esteem changes during a lifetime?

   a. It continues to rise throughout the person's life.
   b. It begins high, but decreases throughout a person's life.
   c. It begins high, then gets lower and higher throughout a person's life.

2 Read lines 3–6. **Likens** means

   a. enjoys
   b. compares
   c. excites

3 In the first paragraph, which word is a synonym for **plunge?**

   _____

4 Read line 8. **Edging toward** means

    a. becoming sharper

    b. moving close to

    c. getting older

5 In line 11, **launched** means

    a. begun

    b. finished

    c. dropped

6 Read lines 16–17. Aly believes that teenagers

    a. feel good about themselves

    b. have negative feelings about themselves

    c. have high self-esteem

7 Read lines 18–20.

    a. **Spearheaded** means

        1. led

        2. attacked

        3. joined

    b. Robins said that "the drop in old age is a little bit more **novel."** He means that the drop in self-esteem in old age is more

        1. like a book

        2. unusual

        3. expected

8 Read lines 22–24.

    a. **Accumulation** means

        1. building up

        2. series of

        3. number of

    b. **Transition** means

        1. unhappiness

        2. change

        3. aging

9 Read line 25. **Those** refers to

   a. the people who responded to the survey
   b. the people who wrote the survey
   c. the people who mailed out the survey

10 In lines 34–36, **superficial information** and **actual achievements** are

   a. opposite ideas
   b. similar ideas

11 In line 37, **fare** means

   a. work
   b. manage
   c. grow

12 Read lines 43–45.

   a. **Blossom** means

     1. develop well
     2. grow flowers
     3. get taller

   b. **Bottom out** means

     1. reach a very high point
     2. reach a very low point
     3. change greatly

13 Read lines 46–50. Which word in these sentences is a synonym of **upswing?**

_____

14 Read lines 63–64. Which one of the following statements is true?

   a. Both adolescents and seniors experience the same sense of loss.
   b. Adolescents experience a sense of loss, but seniors do not.
   c. Adolescents and seniors experience a different sense of loss.

15 In line 69, **in jeopardy** means

   a. in danger
   b. about to change
   c. in question

Information Organization

Read the article again. The author compares the stages of self-esteem to a roller-coaster ride. Turn your book, and write the different stages of a person's self-esteem in the arrows on the chart below. Then write reasons for each stage.

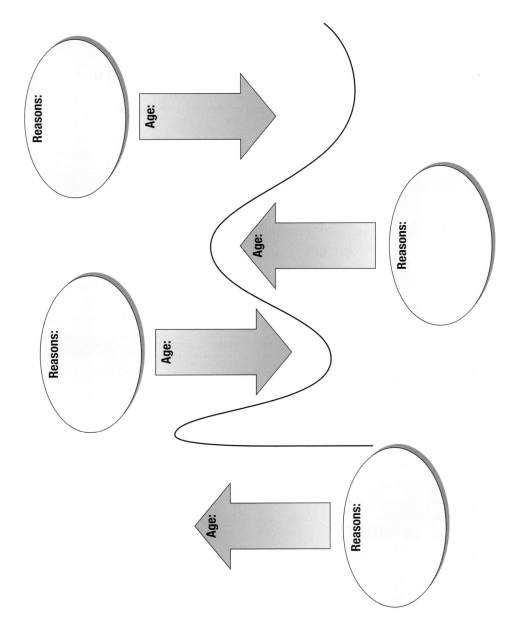

Information Organization Quiz and Summary

Read each question carefully. Use your chart to answer the questions. Do not refer back to the text. When you are finished, write a brief summary of the article.

1 What are the different stages of self-esteem that most people go through?

a. _____

b. _____

c. _____

d. _____

2 For each stage, what happens in people's lives to cause these changes in self-esteem?

a. _____

_____

b. _____

_____

c. _____

_____

d. _____

_____

Summary

_____

_____

_____

_____

_____

_____

Dictionary Skills

Read the dictionary entry for each word. Then look at how the word is used in the sentence. Write the number of the correct definition and the synonym or meaning in the space provided. Remember that you may need to change the wording of the definition in order to have a grammatically correct sentence.

1 | **impact** *n.* **1** a forceful contact: *The meteor made a large impact when it crashed to earth.* **2** effect, impression: *Poverty has a bad impact on people's health.* —*v.infrml.* [I; T] to affect: *Lack of food impacted the starving nation.*

A study suggested that a person's age and stage of life may have a bigger

(   ) _____ on self-esteem than we ever realized.

2 | **inflate** *v.* **-flated, -flating, -flates** **1** [I; T] to fill with air: *A mechanic inflated the car's tires.* **2** [T] to raise above the normal or proper level: *During shortages, some merchants inflate prices.* **3** *fig.* [T] to pump up, swell: *Praise inflates his ego.*

A study of about 350,000 people likens a person's self-esteem across the human lifespan to a roller-coaster ride, starting with a(n)

(   ) _____ sense of self-approval in late childhood that plunges in adolescence.

3 | **scale** *n.* **1** [C] an instrument for weighing things: *I weighed six apples on the scale.* || *According to the scale, I've lost four pounds.* **2** [C; U] a system of measurement or comparison: *On a scale of 1 to 10, I rate this film a 7, quite good.* **3** [C] on a map, a small chart that shows the actual distance: *The scale for this map is 1 inch equals 100 miles.* **4** [C] (in music) a set of notes with the same interval between each one: *She played a C-major scale on the piano. . .*

The survey asked people to agree or strongly disagree—on a five-point

(   ) _____ —with the statement "I see myself as someone who has high self-esteem."

4 | **vulnerable** *adj.* **1** exposed, unprotected: *The soldiers were in a position vulnerable to attack by the enemy.* **2** likely to be hurt or made to feel bad: *She has been feeling very vulnerable since her husband died.*

Fred is aware that his sense of self-esteem may be

(   ) _____ when he retires.

Word Forms

In English, the verb and noun forms of some words are the same, for example, *experience (n.)* and *experience (v.)*.

Complete each sentence with the correct form of the word on the left. **Use the correct tense of the verb in either the affirmative or the negative form. Use the singular or plural form of the noun. In addition, indicate which form you are using by circling *(n.)* for noun or *(v.)* for verb.**

drop

1 During the night, the temperature _____ by
 *(n., v.)*

30 degrees. It was only 26 degrees outside when we woke

up! The sudden _____ in temperature had
 *(n., v.)*

not been predicted, so we were all very surprised.

gain

2 Harry practiced the piano every day. Over several months,

he _____ considerable skill and confidence.
 *(n., v.)*

Because of Harry's _____ in both skill and
 *(n., v.)*

confidence, he was able to play in public.

plunge

3 The newspaper predicted a tremendous _____
 *(n., v.)*

in oil prices over the next several months. Because oil

prices _____ recently, the price of gasoline
 *(n., v.)*

dropped, too.

survey

④ When Anna planned her detailed _____ on
                                        (n., v.)

self-esteem, she did not include children under the age of 12.

She _____ younger children because she was
         (n., v.)

uncomfortable asking them such personal questions.

range

⑤ The students in my school come from a wide

_____ of countries and speak numerous
         (n., v.)

languages. The languages they speak _____
                                          (n., v.)

from Korean, Japanese, Mandarin, Cantonese, Tagalog, and

Vietnamese to Hindi, Farsi, German, French, and Spanish.

PART 2

In English, some verbs change to nouns by adding *-tion* or *-ion*, for example, *collect (v.), collection (n.).*

Complete each sentence with a correct form of the words on the left. Be careful of spelling changes. **Use the correct tense of the verb in either the affirmative or the negative form. Use the singular or plural form of the nouns.**

suggest *(v.)*

suggestion *(n.)*

① Michelle wanted to get a full-time job, but her

friend _____ that she wait until

she finishes school. Michelle listened to her friend's

_____ . She finished school, and then went

to work full time.

participate *(v.)*

participation *(n.)*

② Janet _____ in the school play next week.

She is sorry about her lack of _____ , but

she has to go out of town for an interview.

accumulate (v.)

accumulation (n.)

3 Susan has a surprising _____ of newspapers in her basement. She _____ so many newspapers because she never throws them out. It's a real fire hazard!

realize (v.)

realization (n.)

4 I _____ how hard Maria works until last week. I came to this _____ when I spent the day with her in her office.

contribute (v.)

contribution (n.)

5 John always _____ to class discussions. His thoughtful _____ are always interesting.

Word Partnership	Use *realize* with:
adv.	**suddenly** realize, **finally** realize, **fully** realize
v.	**come to** realize, **make** *someone* realize, **begin to** realize, **fail to** realize
n.	realize **a dream**, realize *your* **potential**

Word Partnership	Use *contribution* with:
adj.	**important** contribution, **significant** contribution
v.	**make a** contribution, **send a** contribution

G

Critical Thinking Strategies

Read each question carefully, and write a response. Remember that there is no one correct answer. Your response depends on what **you** think.

1 The author states that "There is an accumulation of losses occurring all at once, both in old age and adolescence." What losses do you think occur at these two stages of our lives? Why do you think so?

_____

_____

_____

2 According to Richard Robins, we all face certain passages at different times in our lives. What might some of these passages be for adolescents? For adults? Why do these passages occur at these particular points in our lives?

_____

_____

_____

3 In terms of self-esteem, adolescent girls do not manage as well as adolescent boys. Why is body image such a focus for girls, as opposed to boys? Is this focus beginning to change for boys? Why or why not?

_____

_____

_____

4 Richard Robins describes Eileen's experiences (lines 43–50) as a young girl emerging into adulthood. Are her experiences a good example of the kinds of changes that most adolescents go through? Why or why not?

_____

_____

_____

5 At the end of the article, Robins says that he hopes this study will make us more aware of times when our self-esteem may be in danger. Why might this be important for us to know?

_____

_____

_____

H Topics for Discussion and Writing

1 What are some ways that adolescents can maintain their sense of self-esteem in spite of the losses they experience? What advice would you give an adolescent who is suffering a drop in self-esteem?

2 Seniors experience many losses: they retire, and so lose their jobs; loved ones die; their health may deteriorate. What are some ways that seniors can cope with some of these losses?

3 **Write in your journal.** The author compares the stages of self-esteem in our lives to a roller coaster. Do you think this is an accurate comparison? Why or why not? What analogy would you use to describe your own stages of self-esteem?

Follow-Up Activities

1 According to Richard Robins, self-esteem is affected by biological, social, and situational factors. Work with a partner or in a small group. Discuss which biological, social, and situational factors might affect people at each stage of life. Use the chart below to organize your ideas.

	Childhood	Adolescence	Young Adulthood	Adulthood
Biological Factors				
Social Factors				
Situational Factors				

Cloze Quiz

Complete the passage with words from the list. Use each word only once.

accumulation	disagrees	launched	social
adolescence	dropped	likens	spearheaded
adulthood	edging	passage	survey
blossom	fare	plunges	transition
bottomed out	inflated	self-esteem	upswing

No one in the Gould family of Westlake Village, Calif., was surprised by a study suggesting a person's age and stage of life may have a bigger impact on self-esteem than we ever realized. A study of about 350,000 people _____ (1) a person's self-esteem across the human lifespan to a roller-coaster ride, starting with an _____ (2) sense of self-approval in late childhood that _____ (3) in adolescence. Self-esteem rises steadily through adulthood, only to drop to its lowest point ever in old age. "I've gone through pretty much all of those cycles," Fred Gould said. At 60, he's _____ (4) toward retirement. Fred's wife, Eileen, 46, is a businesswoman in the throes of mid-adulthood and, according to the study, predisposed to a healthy self-regard. At 21, the Goulds' son, Jeff, has just _____ (5) that heady climb into _____ (6) and a buoyant self-regard after an _____ (7) fraught with the usual perils of self-doubt and hormonal warfare. His sister, Aly, 17, _____ (8) with a lot of the study, believing instead that each individual has an intrinsic sense of _____ (9) that remains relatively constant. But she does agree that adolescence can give even the most solid sense of self-esteem a sound battering.

The Study

The drop in self-esteem in adolescence was no surprise to Richard Robins, a psychology professor at the University of California at Davis who _____ the study, but "the drop in old age is a little bit more novel," (10) he said. Specifically, Robins was intrigued by the similarities in self-esteem levels between those entering adolescence and old age. "There is an _____ (11) of losses occurring all at once, both in old age and adolescence," he suggested. "There is a critical mass of _____ going on." (12)

Those answering the survey ranged in age from 9 to 90. They participated in the _____ by logging onto a Web site during a period (13) between 1999 and 2000. The survey simply asked people to agree or strongly disagree—on a five-point scale—with the statement: "I see myself as someone who has high self-esteem."

Everybody is an individual, Robins stressed, so self-esteem can be affected by a number of things that are biological, _____ , (14) and situational, but there are certain passages that all of us face—and each _____ can have a powerful effect on our sense of self. (15)

Overall, the study indicated that women do not _____ as (16) well as men in self-esteem—a difference particularly marked in adolescence. "During adolescence, girls' self-esteem _____ about twice as (17) much as boys'," Robins said, perhaps at least partially because of society's heavy emphasis on body image for girls. Add one negative life event to all of this turmoil and a teenager's delicate self-esteem can crumble.

Emerging into Adulthood

Eileen remembered having fairly high self-esteem from ages 12 to 16. She had been very ill as a child, so the teen years were a time for her to

_____ . Then her mother died when she was 17, and her self-esteem _____ . "I was like, 'What do I do? How do I handle this?'" Eileen remembered. Eileen was 22 when she married Fred, an event that coincided with the beginning of her adult years—and an _____ in her self-esteem. Like many adults, Eileen gained her senses of competence and continuity, both of which can contribute to the rise in self-esteem during the adult years, Robins said.

<small>(18)</small> <small>(19)</small> <small>(20)</small>

UNIT 2 | REVIEW

Crossword Puzzle

Read the clues on the next page. Write the answers in the correct spaces in the puzzle.

Crossword Puzzle Clues

ACROSS CLUES

1. A doctor who studies the heart
6. An _____ is an illness.
8. The opposite of **down**
12. The period between 13 and 19 years old
14. Danger
15. **Ours, yours,** _____
17. Make a suggestion
19. A life force
20. Enough; sufficient
22. Include
23. Damage
25. Arrive at a belief or opinion
26. Start up; begin

DOWN CLUES

2. The past tense of **read**
3. Indirect suggestions
4. Attempt
5. To suddenly drop or decrease
7. Compare to
9. The people in a study; the subjects
10. The past tense of **has**
11. Hurry
13. When something is funny, we _____ .
16. A change
18. In vain
21. To be unsuccessful
24. Ann has one _____ and two daughters.

Discussion

1. Even though we live in a modern world, we are still faced with basic threats to our physical and mental health, for example, illness, pain, and loss of self-esteem. Discuss what you think is the biggest threat to you. What is the biggest threat to your family? What can you and your family do about these threats?

2. In Chapter 4, people learn to use laughter to protect themselves from heart disease. In Chapter 5, the author turned to acupuncture, a traditional treatment for pain, after modern medicine did not work. In Chapter 6, the author discusses many factors involved in loss of self-esteem at different points in our lives, but he does not offer any solutions. What solutions might there be to help prevent loss of self-esteem?

The Federal System of Government

by Patricia C. Acheson, *from Our Federal Government: How It Works*

Prereading Preparation

1 How did the United States become an independent country?

2 **a.** Who were the first Europeans in the United States?
   b. Why did they come to the United States?

3 **a.** What kind of government does the United States have?
   b. What do you know about this type of government?

4 What is a **constitution?** Why do governments have constitutions? What is their usual purpose?

5 Take a survey in your class. On the board, write the name of the country each student is from. Then write the type of government each country has. Which countries have the same type of government? Which countries have the same type of government as the United States?

The Federal System of Government

What is the government of the United States exactly? How and when did it come to be? Who were the people who agreed to accept our government and why did they want to accept it?

The answers to these questions lie in the events that took place between 1775 and 1787. In 1775, the war against British domination began. At that point there was no central American government established by law. There was only the Continental Congress made up of men who believed in independence and who were willing to fight for their cause. It was that Congress that declared the colonies independent of Great Britain in July 1776, and it was only after that decision that the evolution of our present form of government began. The initial step was to establish legal governments in the states to replace colonial rule. The states established republics; each of the thirteen new states had elected governors and representative assemblies.

The Continental Congress was without legal foundation, and it was necessary to establish some form of overall government agreed to by the people and speaking for all the states. However, the Americans of this period reluctantly accepted this necessity, as the majority believed that they could guarantee their freedom only if each state remained almost entirely independent of the others.

Therefore, the first government of the United States under the Articles of Confederation adopted in 1781 was very restricted in its authority. It consisted of a Congress made up of representatives from the states. There was no president with certain specific powers, only a chairman whose job it was to preside and to keep order. The Congress had very little power to do anything. Congress could not pass tax laws; it did not have the sole authority to coin money for use by the states, nor could it regulate trade between the states. Because it had no money of its own, the Congress could not pay any of its debts, it could not borrow money, and it could not pay an army or a navy.

Within four years after the end of the war in 1783, it became obvious that the system of government under the Articles of Confederation was not working out. The discontent and the fact that the new nation was extraordinarily weak without an adequate army or navy made thoughtful people realize that a better government must be worked out if the United States of America was to be a strong and rich nation. In Philadelphia in 1787, a convention, or meeting, was held in order to reshape the government. It was there that our present system of government was born, and the Constitution of the United States was written. The people of the United States are still governed today by the framework drawn up in that document over two hundred years ago.

The Constitution

The foreword to the Constitution stated the democratic principles to be followed by the United States government. The government must insure freedom for the citizens of the United States for all time.

To create such a government was not an easy thing to do. Remember that in 1787 the men at the convention in Philadelphia were pioneers in the setting up of a democratic republican government. They really only knew what they did not want. They did not want a king, and they did not want too strong a central government because they were afraid of losing their own freedoms. They certainly wanted to keep the states as they were. To erase them would have been impossible. Each colony had its own individuality and pride. There could be no question of making just one government and forgetting the individual states. On the other hand, the men in Philadelphia knew that the first government set up under the Articles of Confederation had had too little power to carry out its business, and no one had been satisfied.

Here was a dilemma. On the one hand, it seemed that a strong central government was very undesirable because it might endanger the people's liberties. On the other hand, a weak central government had proven inadequate. The solution these men found is called the "system of checks and balances," and it is the heart and soul of the Constitution.

The System of Checks and Balances

The writers of the Constitution wanted to make sure that the people's rights would always be safe and that the central or federal government would never become too powerful. A government ought to have three major powers: to make laws, to carry out those laws, and to provide justice under law for the best interests of the people. Should these three functions be in the hands of one person or one group, there would be great danger that that person or group could use the power for personal profit rather than for the people. To guard against this possibility, the Constitution provided for three major branches of government: the legislature, or congress, to make laws; the executive to carry out the laws; and the judiciary to watch over the rights of the people as described in the Constitution.

The powers of these three branches of the government are described carefully in the Constitution. To make sure that the government should never take more power than it was granted in the Constitution, it was carefully stated that any power not given to the government should forever belong to the states. Another reason for describing carefully the powers of the three branches was to prevent any one branch from becoming stronger than the others. Each job in the running of the country was balanced between the legislative, the executive and the judicial branches. Each part of the government can only function in relation to the others. This system not only balances power between the three branches, but also provides a check on each branch by the others. A good example of the check system can be found in the manner in which laws become laws. The legislature, or Congress, has the job of drafting laws for the country. Once a bill[1] has been passed by the two houses, the Senate and the House of Representatives, the Congress must send a copy to the chief executive, the president of the United States, for his approval. He then has several options as to what he may do. For instance, he may agree with the bill and sign the copy, in which case the law goes into effect. Or, if he should feel that it is not a good law, he may veto it. Vetoing means that he refuses to sign. Should he do that, the copy is returned to the house of Congress in which it originated. If the Congress, sure that the proposed law is a necessary one, passes it again by a two-thirds majority, the bill becomes a law regardless of the president's veto. The people are represented in Congress, and if they still favor the law, it is more democratic that they should have it.

The checks system goes further. The judicial branch has its say about the laws of the land. Once the Congress and the president have agreed upon a law, it must be enforced all over the United States. If someone disagrees with a federal law and challenges it by disobeying it, the case is brought into the court system of the United States. If the Supreme Court decides to hear the case, it has the duty of examining the law and determining if it is constitutional, or in other words, whether the law is in keeping with the rights of the people as outlined in the Constitution.

This system of balanced power and of checks between the branches of the government means that at all times the people's rights and interests are being carefully guarded. It must be stressed, however, that as Thomas Jefferson[2] said, "Eternal vigilance is the price of liberty," and if the people of the United States, their elected representatives, and their judges are not constantly vigilant, no mere words on paper are going to protect their freedom.

[1] A bill is the name given to a law before it is signed by the president.
[2] Thomas Jefferson was the principal writer of the Declaration of Independence and the third president of the United States.

Fact-Finding Exercise

Read the passage again. Then read the following statements. Scan the article quickly to see if they are True (T) or False (F). If a statement is false, rewrite it so that it is true.

1   T   F   The United States became independent in 1775.

_____

2   T   F   The first U.S. government did not have a president.

_____

3   T   F   The United States' present government began in 1787.

_____

4 _____ T _____ F   The U.S. Constitution described two branches of the government: the legislative and the judicial.

_____

5 _____ T _____ F   The system of checks and balances prevents one branch of government from becoming too powerful.

_____

6 _____ T _____ F   If the president disagrees with a new bill, it can never become a law.

_____

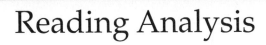

B Reading Analysis

Read each question carefully. Circle the number or letter of the correct answer, or write your answer in the space provided.

1 Read lines 5–6. What does **at that point** mean?

   a. 1775

   b. 1787

   c. Between 1775 and 1787

2 Read lines 6–10.

   a. What was the men's **cause?**

   _____

   b. In line 8, what does **that Congress** refer to?

   _____

3 Read lines 10–12.

   a. **Initial** means

     1. a letter of the alphabet

     2. the first

     3. the most difficult

b. Rule means

    1. law

    2. state

    3. colony

c. This sentence means that the people wanted to

    1. start new governments instead of the colonial government

    2. establish the colonial government again

    3. get rid of all forms of government

4 Read lines 14–16. "The Continental Congress was without legal foundation . . ." This sentence means that

  a. the Continental Congress broke the law

  b. the Continental Congress did not make laws

  c. the Continental Congress had no legal authority

5 Read lines 16–20.

  a. In line 16, **reluctantly** means

    1. recently

    2. unanimously

    3. unwillingly

  b. Complete the following sentence:

    Gary wanted to find a job in New York because he thinks it is an exciting city. When he was unable to find a job there, he reluctantly

    1. accepted a job in New Jersey

    2. continued looking for a job

  c. In line 17, **majority** means

    1. some of the people

    2. more than half of the people

    3. all of the people

  d. In line 19, **therefore** means

    1. furthermore

    2. in addition

    3. as a result

6 In line 22, **whose** refers to

  a. the president

  b. the chairman

  c. the Congress

7 Read lines 23–27. What types of control was the Congress not given?

_____

_____

_____

8 Read lines 30–33.

    a. **Discontent** means

        1. discomfort
        2. dissatisfaction
        3. disagreement

    b. Why were the people discontented?

_____

9 In line 42, **pioneers** are people who

    a. create new systems of government
    b. set things up based on what they do not want
    c. do something that no one has ever done before

10 Read lines 52–56.

    a. What is a **dilemma?**

        1. It is a problem with two possible good solutions.
        2. It is a problem with two difficulties and one good solution.
        3. It is a problem with two possible solutions, neither of which is perfect.

    b. What follows **on the one hand** and **on the other hand?**

        1. The two possible solutions to the problem
        2. Two good solutions to the problem
        3. Two bad solutions to the problem

    c. What is the **heart and soul of the Constitution?**

_____

11 Read lines 61–63. What are **hands?**

    a. Law
    b. Control
    c. Body parts

12 Read lines 79–82.

    a. What is a **bill?**

    _____

    b. How do you know?

    _____

    c. This type of information is called a

    _____

13 Read lines 84–88.

    a. What does **veto** mean?

    _____

    b. In line 88, **regardless of** means

      1. in addition to
      2. because of
      3. in spite of

    c. Complete the following sentence:

    Thomas wanted to go to the beach with his friends. He heard on the radio that it might rain in the afternoon. He decided to go to the beach regardless of

      1. the weather report
      2. his friends

14 Read lines 100–103.

    a. Who was Thomas Jefferson?

    _____

    b. Where did you find this information?

    _____

C Information Organization

Read the article again. Underline what you think are the main ideas. Then scan the article and complete the following outline, using the sentences that you have underlined to help you. You will use this outline later to answer specific questions about the article.

I. The Origin of the Federal System of Government

   A. _____

   B. *The Continental Congress existed, but had no legal power*

   C. *Legal governments in the states were established to replace colonial rule*

   D. _____

II. _____

    A. Its purpose:

    B. The feelings of the writers of the Constitution:

        1. _____

        2. *They did not want a strong central government* _____

        3. _____

        4. _____

III. _____

    A. The purpose of this system:

        1. _____

        2. _____

        3. _____

    B. *The powers not given to the government belong to the states* _____

    C. _____

IV. _____

    A. *The legislature, or Congress, drafts a law* _____

    B. _____

    C. _____

        1. _____

        2. _____

    D. *If someone challenges the law, the judicial branch determines whether the law is constitutional or not*

Information Organization
Quiz and Summary

Read each question carefully. Use your notes to answer the questions. Do not refer back to the text. When you are finished, write a brief summary of the article.

1 **a.** What kind of government did the United States have before the Constitution was written?

_____

_____

b. Was this government successful? Why, or why not?

_____

_____

2 What features of government didn't the writers of the Constitution want?

_____

_____

3 **a.** What is the purpose of the system of checks and balances?

_____

_____

b. How does it work?

_____

_____

4 How are laws made in the United States?

_____

_____

Summary

_____

_____

_____

_____

_____

Dictionary Skills

Read the dictionary entry for each word. Then look at how the word is used in the sentence. Write the number of the correct definition and the synonym or meaning in the space provided. Remember that you may need to change the wording of the definition in order to have a grammatically correct sentence.

1 | **cause** *n* **1** **a** : a reason for an action or condition : motive **b** : something that brings about an effect or a result **c** : a person or thing that is the occasion of an action or state; *especially* : an agent that brings something about **d** : sufficient reason <discharged for *cause*> **2** **a** : a ground of legal action **b** : case **3** : a matter or question to be decided **4** **a** : a principle or movement militantly defended or supported **b** : a charitable undertaking <for a good *cause*>

The Continental Congress was made up of men who believed

in independence and who believed very strongly in the

(   ) _____ that they supported.

2 | **assembly** *n* **1** : a company of persons gathered for deliberation and legislation, worship, or entertainment **2** : *capitalized* : a legislative body; *specif* : the lower house of a legislature **3** : a meeting of a student body and usually faculty for administrative, educational, or recreational purposes . . . **5** : a signal for troops to assemble or fall in . . .

The thirteen new states had elected governors and representative

(   ) _____ .

By permission. From *Merriam-Webster's Collegiate® Dictionary*, 11th Edition ©2010 by Merriam-Webster, Incorporated (www.Merriam-Webster.com).

It would have been impossible to (   ) _____ the individual states.

Word Forms

PART 1

In English, some adjectives become nouns by deleting the final -*t* and adding -*ce*, for example, *competent (adj.), competence (n.)*.
    Complete each sentence with the correct form of the words on the left. **Use the singular form of the nouns.**

reluctant *(adj.)*   **1** Charles felt quite _____ about driving alone

reluctance *(n.)*   from New York to Chicago to attend a conference. We all

           understood his unwillingness to travel so far by himself.

           Because of his _____ to drive alone, he

           decided to take the train instead.

vigilant *(adj.)*   **2** It has rained so little in California for the last six years that

vigilance *(n.)*   forest rangers need to be especially _____

           in watching for forest fires. Unfortunately, in spite of their

           around-the-clock _____ , fires have started

           and gotten out of control, causing the loss of thousands of

           acres of forest.

resistant *(adj.)* ③ My grandparents are quite _____ to any

resistance *(n.)* kind of change. Sometimes their _____ is

humorous. For example, they refuse to buy a new car, even

though theirs is 30 years old and always breaks down when

they drive into town. When the phone rings on Saturday

morning, we always know who it is.

distant *(adj.)* ④ Because Julie lives a long _____ from

distance *(n.)* her parents, she calls them every Sunday evening.

Unfortunately, last night the connection was very poor;

their voices sounded so _____ that Julie

hung up and tried the call again.

PART 2

In English, verbs can change to nouns in several ways. Some verbs become
nouns by adding the suffix *-ment*, for example, *equip (v.), equipment (n.).*
    Complete each sentence with the correct form of the words on the left.
**Use the correct tense of the verbs, in either the affirmative or the negative
form. Use the singular or plural form of the nouns.**

replace *(v.)* ① When my car broke down, I took it to the mechanic, who

replacement *(n.)* said that the carburetor needed a _____ . He

not only _____ the carburetor, but he also

tuned up the engine, and it cost me $900!

pay *(v.)* ② At registration, Phoebe _____ the full cost

payment *(n.)* of her tuition at once. She arranged to cover her tuition in

several _____ over four months.

enforce *(v.)*
enforcement *(n.)*

3 Rebecca is doing a study on law _____ for her master's thesis. She has discovered that some police precincts _____ the law as effectively as other precincts do.

establish *(v.)*
establishment *(n.)*

4 Next year, the university _____ a new scholarship fund for foreign students. The permanent _____ of this type of scholarship fund will enable more students to study in this country.

agree *(v.)*
agreement *(n.)*

5 Tony _____ with us about going to the movies last night. In fact, we had an argument about it. We finally reached a mutual _____ after we found a movie that Tony really wanted to see.

Word Partnership	Use *establish* with:
n.	establish **control**, establish **independence**, establish **rules**, establish **contact**, establish **relations**, establish *someone's* **identity**

Word Partnership	Use *agreement* with:
n.	**peace** agreement, **terms of an** agreement, **trade** agreement
v.	**enter into an** agreement, **sign an** agreement, **reach an** agreement

Critical Thinking Strategies

Read each question carefully, and write a response. Remember that there is no one correct answer. Your response depends on what **you** think.

1 Read the first paragraph. Why does the article begin with a series of questions? In other words, what do you think is the author's purpose in asking the reader questions at the beginning of the reading passage?

_____

_____

_____

_____

2 Read lines 43–47. Why do you think these people were so sure about what kind of government they did *not* want?

_____

_____

_____

_____

3 Read the description of the system of checks and balances in lines 57–97. Do you think that this system adequately protects the people's rights and that it prevents the federal government from becoming too powerful? Explain your answer.

_____

_____

_____

_____

4 Read lines 59–61: "A government ought to have three major powers: to make laws, to carry out those laws, and to provide justice under law for the best interests of the people." Do you agree or disagree with this statement? That is, do you think these should be the major powers of any government? Explain your answer.

_____

_____

_____

_____

5 After reading this selection, specifically lines 16–18, 44–48, and 68–71, what can you understand about the individuality of the states in the United States? For instance, how do you think that the fact that the United States is divided into states affects American culture and the attitudes of the people in each state?

_____

_____

_____

_____

Topics for Discussion and Writing

1 Alone or with classmates from your country, write a description of the form of government in your country. Compare it with the form of government in the United States. For example, how are laws made? Who is the leader of the country? How is he or she granted this position? Compare your country's form of government with those of the other students' countries.

2 **Write in your journal.** Is there something that the writers of the Constitution overlooked in the system of checks and balances that you think is important? In other words, did they forget to include a check or balance that you think is necessary to help control the federal government and keep it from becoming too powerful? Explain your answer.

Follow-Up Activities

1 **Jigsaw Reading:** You are going to read about the three branches of the U.S. government: the legislative branch, the executive branch, and the judicial branch.

   a. First, read the paragraph entitled *The System of Checks and Balances* below. Discuss it in class to make sure everyone understands it.

   b. Second, work in a group of three or four students. Each group will read about one branch of government on the following pages. Group A will read about the legislative branch, Group B will read about the executive branch, and Group C will read about the judicial branch. After reading the paragraph, discuss it to make sure everyone in the group understands about their particular branch.

   c. Third, set up different groups so that each group has a student or students who have read about the three different branches. In these new groups, tell each other what you have read about each branch. Take notes about the other two readings. Do not look back at your readings. Ask each other questions to make sure that all the students in your group understand how the three branches work.

   d. Finally, work together to complete the Federal System of Government Chart on page 140. When your group is finished, compare your chart with the other groups' charts.

The System of Checks and Balances

The writers of the Constitution wanted to make sure that the people's rights would always be safe and that the federal government would never become too powerful. Therefore, the writers of the Constitution set up three branches of government: the legislature, or Congress, to make laws; the executive branch—the president—to carry out the laws; the judicial branch, to watch over the rights of the people. The system of checks and balances makes sure that one branch cannot become stronger than another. This system not only balances power among the three branches but also provides a check on each branch by the others.

Group A Only: The Legislative Branch

The legislative branch, or Congress, represents all states fairly. It consists of two parts: the House of Representatives and the Senate. The vice president of the United States acts as the president of the Senate. Each state has two senators, who are elected every six years. The number of members in the House of Representatives depends on the population of each state[1]. Representatives are elected every two years. To be elected as a senator, a person must be at least 30-years-old, have been a citizen for nine years, and be a resident of the state she/he will represent. To be elected as a representative, a person must be at least 25-years-old, have been a citizen for seven years, and be a resident of the state she/he will represent.

The major job of the Congress is to make laws. If the president vetoes, or rejects, a proposed law, the Congress can pass the law anyway by getting a two-thirds majority vote. Congress can also declare war by getting a two-thirds majority vote of the senators and representatives. The House of Representatives can also impeach the president. This means that the House can charge the president with a crime. In this case, the Senate will put the president on trial, so the vice president must resign as the president of the Senate. The Senate votes to approve the justices that the president appoints to the Supreme Court. These are just a few of the legislative branch's many responsibilities.

Group B's Information:

_____

_____

_____

_____

_____

_____

Group C's Information:

_____

_____

_____

_____

_____

_____

[1] The House of Representatives has 435 members.

Group B Only: The Executive Branch

The executive branch of the government puts the country's laws into effect. The president of the United States is a member of the executive branch. The president must be at least 35 years old and be a natural citizen of the United States. In addition, he must have lived in the United States for at least 14 years and be a civilian. The president is elected every four years and cannot serve more than two terms in a row. The vice president acts as president of the Senate. When the president receives a bill from Congress, he must sign it in order for it to become a law. However, if he disagrees with the law, he can veto, or reject, it. The president can also ask the Congress to declare war. He also appoints the justices to the Supreme Court. He must do his job according to the Constitution, or he may be impeached, that is, charged with a crime by Congress. The executive branch is a very important part of the U.S. government and must work with the other two branches according to the Constitution.

Group A's Information:

_____

_____

_____

_____

_____

_____

_____

_____

_____

Group C's Information:

_____

_____

_____

_____

_____

_____

_____

_____

_____

_____

Group C Only: The Judicial Branch

The judicial branch of government is the system of courts in the United States. Its job is to enforce the laws. The Supreme Court is the highest court in the country. It consists of nine justices: one chief justice and eight associate justices. The Constitution does not state any specific requirements for Supreme Court positions. The president appoints the justices, but the Senate must approve them. The justices are appointed for life. The Supreme Court not only makes sure that people obey the laws but can also declare a law unconstitutional. In other words, the Supreme Court can decide if a law is not in agreement with the Constitution. Furthermore, the chief justice acts as president of the Senate if there is an impeachment trial. In an impeachment trial, the Congress charges the president of the United States with a crime. The judicial branch works together with the legislative and executive branches to protect the Constitution and the rights of the people.

Group A's Information:

_____

_____

_____

_____

_____

_____

_____

_____

Group B's Information:

_____

_____

_____

_____

_____

_____

_____

_____

2 In your groups, work together to complete the following chart. Do not look back at the paragraphs you have read.

THE FEDERAL SYSTEM OF GOVERNMENT			
	Legislative Branch	Executive Branch	Judicial Branch
Function			
Number of Members	Congress: _____ Senators _____ Representatives	1. 2. (acts as president of the Senate)	Justices: _____ Chief Justice _____ Associate Justices
Term of Office	Senate: House of Representatives:	President:	Justices:
Requirements	Senator: 1. 2. 3. Representative: 1. 2. 3.	President: 1. 2. 3. 4.	
Responsibilities: Laws	1. 2.	President: 1. 2. 3.	
Responsibilities: War		President:	
Impeachment	House of Representatives: Senate:	President: Vice President:	Chief Justice of the Supreme Court:

Cloze Quiz

Complete the passage with words from the list. Use each word only once.

afraid	endanger	king	solution
Constitution	found	men	states
democratic	freedoms	other	strong
dilemma	government	pioneers	too
easy	hand	really	undesirable

To create a government was not an _____ thing to
(1)
do. Remember that in 1787 the _____ at the convention
(2)
in Philadelphia were _____ in the setting up of a
(3)
_____ republican government. They _____ only
(4)   (5)
knew what they did not want. They did not want a _____ , and
(6)
they did not want _____ strong a central government because
(7)
they were _____ of losing their own _____ . They
(8)   (9)
certainly wanted to keep the _____ as they were.
(10)

Here was a _____ . On the one _____ ,
(11)   (12)
it seemed that a _____ central government was very
(13)
_____ because it might _____ the
(14)   (15)
people's liberties. On the _____ hand, a weak central
(16)
_____ had proven inadequate. The _____ these
(17)   (18)
men _____ is called the "system of checks and balances," and
(19)
it is the heart and soul of the _____ .
(20)

8
CHAPTER

Teachers Are Key for Students

by Greg Toppo, *USA TODAY*

Prereading Preparation

1 Look at the pictures and describe the students. What kind of classes do you think these are? Do the students seem interested or bored? Why?

2 Are some classes more interesting than others? What are some reasons for this?

3 Read the title of this chapter. What do you think it means?

4 Work in a small group. Ask and answer the questions in the chart below; then write your answers. Discuss your answers with your class.

Name	What was your favorite class in school?	Why?

Teachers Are Key for Students

1   People are naturally curious, so why is school such a chore for so many kids?
University of Virginia cognitive scientist Daniel Willingham set out to learn why
in his new book, *Why Don't Students Like School?* Part of the answer, he finds, is
that thinking can be just plain hard. Unless conditions are right, we'll actually

5   try to avoid the process of thinking. A teacher's challenge, the author says, is to
"maximize the likelihood that students will get the great feeling rush that comes
from successful thought." The author chats about the learning process.

**Q: After all we've learned about the mind and brain, why is it so difficult to
make school enjoyable for students?**

10 **A:** School is all about mental challenge, and that is hard work, make no
mistake. Still, people do enjoy mental work or, more exactly, people enjoy
successful mental work. We get a snap of satisfaction when we solve a problem.
But solving a problem that is trivially easy is not fun. Neither is hammering
away at a problem with no sense you are making progress.

15 The challenge for a teacher is to find that perfect amount of mental difficulty, and
to find it simultaneously for 25 students, each with a different level of preparation.
To fight this problem, teachers must engage each student with work that is
appropriate for his or her level of preparation. This must be done sensitively, so
that students who are behind don't feel like second-class citizens. However, the fact

20 is they are behind, and pretending that they are not does them no favors.

**Q: You say that "Memory is the residue of thought." Why do we remember
what we remember?**

A: It would be great if you simply remembered what you wanted to remember;
you'd remember everyone's name at parties, and you'd never misplace your

25 keys. But obviously memory doesn't work that way. Rather, we remember what
we think about, and that can have non-obvious consequences. During frog
dissection, are students thinking about anatomy or that they find it gross?

One way to help ensure that students think of content is to view teaching in
terms of a story structure. Stories draw us in (and are easy to remember) because

30 they constantly pose small, solvable mental problems that invite us to interpret
the action and predict what will happen next: *How will E.T. get home?*

**Q: Ninety percent of people think they're either a visual, auditory or
kinesthetic learner. What does that mean? And why do you say that they are
wrong?**

35 **A:** The idea is that people have different ways of learning the same material,
or learning styles. A visual learner understands and remembers better by seeing,
an auditory learner by hearing, and a kinesthetic learner by touching and

manipulating. This idea has been tested repeatedly in the last 50 years and it doesn't work. People differ in their abilities and in their interests, but there is no evidence for differences in learning styles.

Q: You say that intelligence is much more malleable than most people believe. How can we all get smarter?

A: Until about 20 years ago, most scientists thought that intelligence was mostly inherited, and that the environment's impact was limited. Important findings supporting this view came from studies of identical twins who were separated at birth. Even though adopted into different families, they usually showed very similar intelligence, which indicated that genes dominated.

Now scientists think that those early studies underestimated the effect of the environment. First, adoptive families probably don't vary that much—they are generally supportive and emphasize success in school. Second, other data have shown that moving kids from low-quality to high-quality schools boosts IQ scores.

The secret to getting smarter is really not a big secret: engage in intellectual activities. Read the newspaper, watch informative documentaries, find well-written books that make intellectual content engaging. Perhaps most important: watch less television. It's rarely enriching, and it's an enormous waste of time.

Just as exercise experts advise many small changes rather than a vigorous program (which will likely be dropped), I think the best way to get smarter is to put a little more learning into every day. The trick is to develop the habit of looking for those opportunities.

UNIT 3   GOVERNMENT AND EDUCATION

Fact-Finding Exercise

Read the passage again. Then, read the following statements. Scan the article quickly to see if they are True (T) or False (F). If a statement is false, rewrite it so that it is true.

1. _____ T _____ F Daniel Willingham believes that it's sometimes difficult for students to think.

_____

2. _____ T _____ F We enjoy solving easy problems.

_____

3. _____ T _____ F We remember everything we want to remember.

_____

4. _____ T _____ F People have different learning styles.

_____

5. _____ T _____ F Most scientists today no longer believe that intelligence is mostly inherited.

_____

6. _____ T _____ F It is possible to make yourself smarter.

_____

7. _____ T _____ F According to this article, watching television can make you smarter.

_____

Reading Analysis

Read each question carefully. Circle the number or letter of the correct answer, or write your answer in the space provided.

1 Read the first line of the article. This sentence means that
   a. many kids think school is boring, but necessary
   b. many kids like school because they are curious
   c. many kids think attending school is natural

2 Read line 7. **Chats** means
   a. writes informally
   b. speaks informally
   c. explains in detail

3 Read lines 11–12. People enjoy
   a. solving all kinds of problems
   b. solving problems that are very easy
   c. solving problems that make us feel successful

4 Read lines 13–14. **"Hammering away at a problem with no sense you are making progress"** means
   a. working hard on a problem without feeling successful
   b. working hard on a problem and then solving it
   c. causing a problem that you are unable to solve

5 Read lines 18–19.
   a. A **second-class citizen** refers to someone who
      1. feels poor
      2. feels inferior
      3. feels cheap
   b. In this sentence, **behind** means
      1. less successful than others
      2. sitting in back of someone
      3. more successful than others

6 Read lines 29–31. To **pose a problem** means to

    a. solve a problem
    b. discuss a problem
    c. present a problem

7 **a.** Read lines 48–49. According to scientists, the environment

    1. does have an impact on intelligence
    2. has little or no impact on intelligence
    3. has exactly the same impact on intelligence as genetics

    b. **Underestimate** means

    1. guess correctly
    2. guess incorrectly
    3. guess too low

8 Read lines 50–51. **"Second, other data have shown that moving kids from low-quality to high-quality schools boosts IQ scores."** This statement illustrates

    a. the impact of genes on intelligence
    b. the impact of the environment on intelligence

9 Read lines 52–54. An **intellectual activity** is an activity that

    a. involves reading
    b. involves thinking
    c. involves big secrets

10 Read lines 57–59.

    a. **Many small changes** and **a vigorous program** are

    1. similar ideas
    2. opposite ideas
    3. experts' ideas

    b. What **will likely be dropped?**

    1. Small changes
    2. A new exercise schedule
    3. A vigorous program

Information Organization

Read the article again. Underline what you think are the main ideas. Then scan the article and fill in the chart, using the sentences that you have underlined to help you. You will use this chart later to answer specific questions about the article.

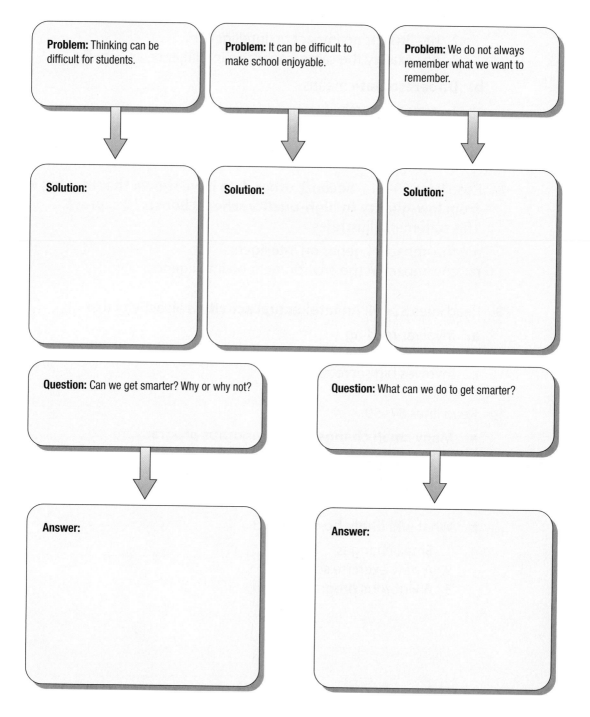

Problem: Thinking can be difficult for students.

Problem: It can be difficult to make school enjoyable.

Problem: We do not always remember what we want to remember.

Solution:

Solution:

Solution:

Question: Can we get smarter? Why or why not?

Question: What can we do to get smarter?

Answer:

Answer:

Information Organization
Quiz and Summary

Read each question carefully. Use your notes and the chart on the previous page to answer the questions. Do not refer back to the text. When you are finished, write a brief summary of the article.

1 What is a teacher's challenge regarding "thinking"?

_____

_____

_____

2 How can teachers make learning enjoyable for students?

_____

_____

_____

3 How can teachers help students remember what they need to remember?

_____

_____

_____

4 **a.** Until about 20 years ago, what did most scientists believe about intelligence?

_____

_____

b. Do they still believe that today? Why or why not?

_____

_____

_____

5 **a.** What does Daniel Willingham suggest we can do with our intelligence?

_____

_____

_____

b. How can we do this?

_____

_____

_____

Summary

_____

_____

_____

_____

_____

_____

_____

_____

Dictionary Skills

Read the dictionary entry for each word. Then look at how the word is used in the sentence. Write the number of the correct definition and the synonym or meaning in the space provided. **Be sure to use the correct form of the verbs and nouns.** Remember that you may need to change the wording of the definition in order to have a grammatically correct sentence.

1 **cognitive** *adj* **1** : of, relating to, being, or involving conscious intellectual activity (as thinking, reasoning, or remembering) **2** : based on or capable of being reduced to empirical factual knowledge

Daniel Willingham, of the University of Virginia, is a

(   ) _____ scientist.

2 **anatomy** *n* **1** : a branch of morphology that deals with the structure of organisms **2** : a treatise on anatomical science or art **3** : the art of separating the parts of an organism in order to ascertain their position, relations, structure, and function : dissection. . . **5** : structural makeup *esp* of an organism or any of its parts **6** : a separating or dividing into parts for detailed examination : analysis. . .

During frog dissection, are students thinking about

(   ) _____ or that they find it gross?

3 **malleable** *adj* **1** : capable of being extended or shaped by beating with a hammer or by the pressure of rollers **2 a** : capable of being altered or controlled by outside forces or influences **b** : having a capacity for adaptive change

You say that intelligence is much more (   ) _____

than most people believe. How can we all get smarter?

F Word Forms

In English, adjectives usually become adverbs by adding the suffix -ly, for example, *similar (adj.), similarly (adv.)*.
Complete each sentence with the correct form of the words on the left.

curious *(adj.)*
curiously *(adv.)*

1 My sandwich _____ disappeared on the beach last week. I soon learned that a _____ seagull had flown down and taken it!

mental *(adj.)*
mentally *(adv.)*

2 Young Sun's final exam was a _____ challenge for her. She studied hard the night before, and _____ prepared herself for the test. As a result, she did very well.

appropriate *(adj.)*
appropriately *(adv.)*

3 It's important to dress _____ for every situation. For example, it is not _____ to wear shorts to a wedding.

sensitive *(adj.)*
sensitively *(adv.)*

4 Dr. Nieto is extremely _____ to all his patients. He discusses their illnesses very _____ so that they feel comfortable speaking with him.

vigorous *(adj.)*
vigorously *(adv.)*

5 Elaine has a _____ exercise routine. She runs five miles every morning in just a half hour! Then she lifts weights for half an hour, showers, and dries herself _____ with a towel—all before going to work!

PART 2

In English, some verbs change to adjectives by adding the suffix - *able,* for example, *enjoy (v.), enjoyable (adj.).*

Complete each sentence with the correct form of the word on the left. **Use the correct tense of the verb in either the affirmative or the negative form.**

avoid *(v.)*

avoidable *(adj.)*

1 Many bicycle accidents are _____ if you ride your bike carefully. You can also _____ getting seriously injured by always wearing a bike helmet.

advise *(v.)*

advisable *(adj.)*

2 Karina _____ her brother to call the movie theater before they left home. Since the movies frequently change at that theater, it is _____ to call ahead of time.

predict *(v.)*

predictable *(adj.)*

3 The weather forecaster _____ rain for yesterday, so Donna didn't bring her umbrella and got soaked. Because the weather is not very _____ at this time of the year, Donna now carries one all the time!

vary *(v.)*

variable *(adj.)*

4 The cafeteria food is always the same in the morning: bread, eggs, and cereal. The lunch menu _____ , either. However, the dinner menu is _____ , so I can eat something different every night.

solve *(v.)*

solvable *(adj.)*

5 Chris easily _____ the difficult calculus problem in class. He's very good in math, so the problem was _____ for him.

Word Partnership	Use *vary* with:
n.	**prices** vary, **rates** vary, **styles** vary, vary **by location,** vary **by size,** vary **by state,** vary **by store**
adv.	vary **considerably,** vary **greatly,** vary **slightly,** vary **widely**

Word Partnership	Use *solve* with:
n.	**ability to** solve *something,* solve **a crisis,** solve **a mystery,** solve **a problem,** solve **a puzzle, way to** solve *something*
v.	**attempt/try to** solve *something,* **help** solve *something*

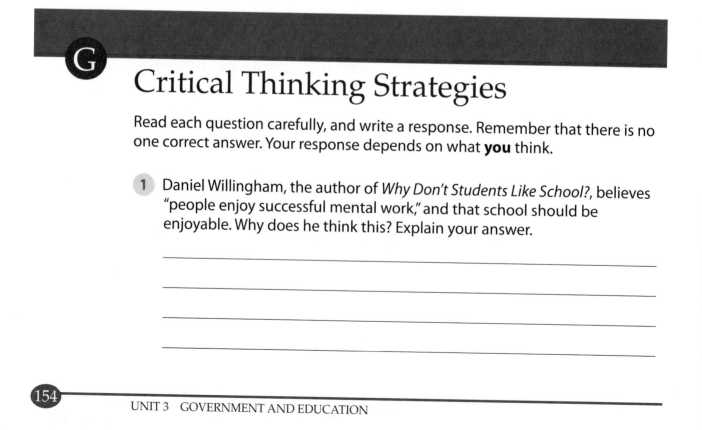

ⒼCritical Thinking Strategies

Read each question carefully, and write a response. Remember that there is no one correct answer. Your response depends on what **you** think.

1 Daniel Willingham, the author of *Why Don't Students Like School?*, believes "people enjoy successful mental work," and that school should be enjoyable. Why does he think this? Explain your answer.

_____

_____

_____

_____

2 According to this article, students remember a story better than a lesson? What do you think is the reason for this?

_____

_____

_____

_____

3 Daniel Willingham suggests we engage in intellectual activities to increase our intelligence. What are "intellectual activities"? Give some examples.

_____

_____

_____

_____

Topics for Discussion and Writing

1 Scientists used to believe that intelligence was mostly inherited, and that the environment's impact was limited. Now scientists think that early studies underestimated the effect of the environment. Which do you believe has a bigger impact on intelligence: your genes or your environment? Why do you think this?

2 What do you think makes a class enjoyable? For example, the subject, the teacher, your classmates, etc. Why?

3 Is it important for a teacher to try to make a class enjoyable? Why or why not?

4 **Write in your journal.** Think about an enjoyable class that you had in high school or college. Why was it enjoyable? What did you learn?

Follow-Up Activities

1. Below is a list of the best study habits of successful students.

   a. Review the previous seven chapters in *Concepts*. For which chapters did you demonstrate a best study habit?

TEN BEST STUDY HABITS OF SUCCESSFUL STUDENTS	
Best Study Habit	Chapters for which I demonstrated this habit
1. Read assigned texts / handouts.	
2. Don't procrastinate.	
3. Pay attention to the organization of the text.	
4. Highlight key ideas and vocabulary in the text as you read.	
5. Review often.	
6. Study with a study group.	
7. Get help before it's too late.	
8. Do homework assignments.	
9. Make an outline or take notes of your reading.	
10. Set aside a quiet place to study with few distractions.	

   b. Which best study habits have you been doing regularly? Which best study habits do you need to develop?

2. According to this article, there are steps you can take to make yourself smarter, such as reading more and watching informative documentaries. What else can you do to become more intelligent? Work with a partner. Make a list together and share it with your classmates. Which suggestions will you follow to help yourself become more intelligent?

Cloze Quiz

J

Complete the passage with words from the list. Use each word only once.

advise	identical	newspaper	smarter
data	impact	opportunities	supportive
effect	important	scientists	though
enormous	informative	secret	vary
genes	intelligence	similar	vigorous

Until about 20 years ago, most scientists thought that _____ (1) was mostly inherited, and that the environment's _____ (2) was limited. Important findings supporting this view came from studies of _____ (3) twins who were separated at birth. Even _____ (4) adopted into different families, they usually showed very _____ (5) intelligence, which indicated that _____ (6) dominated.

Now _____ (7) think that those early studies underestimated the _____ (8) of the environment. First, adoptive families probably don't _____ (9) that much—they are generally _____ (10) and emphasize success in school. Second, other _____ (11) have shown that moving kids from low-quality to high-quality schools boosts IQ scores.

The secret to getting smarter is really not a big _____ (12) : engage in intellectual activities. Read the _____ (13) , watch _____ (14) documentaries, find well-written books that make intellectual content engaging. Perhaps most _____ (15) : watch less television. It's rarely enriching, and it's an _____ (16) waste of time.

Just as exercise experts _____ (17) many small changes rather than a _____ (18) program (which will likely be dropped), I think the best way to get _____ (19) is to put a little more learning into every day. The trick is to develop the habit of looking for those _____ (20) .

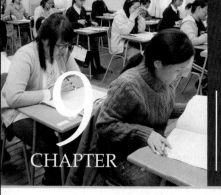

9

CHAPTER

The Pursuit of Excellence
by Jill Smolowe
Time

Prereading Preparation

1. In your country, what are the requirements for a student to attend college? Can any student go to college in your country? Why, or why not?

2. In the United States, what are the requirements for a foreign student to attend college? What are the requirements for an American student to attend college? Can any student go to college?

3. Why did you come to another country to study? Why do you think there are so many foreign students in American universities?

4. Take an in-class survey of the reasons students decide to study in another country.

   a. In a small group, discuss why students might choose to study abroad, e.g., cost, choice of subjects, etc.
   b. In your group, list the reasons you decided to study abroad.
   c. Compare your list with the other groups' lists. What is the most common reason students in your class have for studying abroad? The second most common reason? The third? Save your lists. Later, you will compare these to the responses from another survey you will do.

5. Look at the title of this article. What do you think it means?

Track 09

The Pursuit of Excellence

1   Sometime around the seventh grade, many American students are introduced to the tale of 10 blind men inspecting an elephant. When each blind man reaches different conclusions about the creature, the students are invited to consider whether truth is absolute or lies in the eye of the beholder. College professors and administrators might want to remember that fable when they take the measure of
5 American higher education. Many of them, who tend to see only what they stand to lose, perceive the beast as wounded, suffering from the shocks of rising costs, dwindling resources and life-draining cutbacks. But foreigners, who compare America's universities with their own, often reach very different conclusions
10 about the nature of the beast.
    If sheer numbers provide any proof, America's universities and colleges are the envy of the world. For all their abiding troubles, the United States' 3,500 institutions were flooded with 407,530 students from 193 different countries last year. Asia led the way with 39,600 students from China and 36,610 from Japan,
15 followed by India and Canada. Many of the foreigners entered graduate and undergraduate programs in roughly equal numbers. . . .
    Most European and Asian universities provide an elite service to a small and privileged clientele. While fully 60% of all U.S. high school graduates attend college at some point in their life, just 30% of the comparable German

population, 28% of the French, 20% of the British and 37% of the Japanese proceed beyond high school. German students who survive the *Abitur* or Britons who pass their A levels may still not qualify for a top university at home, but find American universities far more welcoming. Some U.S. schools acknowledge the rigor of European secondary training and will give up to a year's credit to foreigners who have passed their high school exams.

"The egalitarian conception that everyone has a right to an education appropriate to his potential is a highly democratic and compassionate standard," says Marvin Bressler, professor of sociology and education specialist at Princeton University. True, not all U.S. collegians can match the performance of their foreign counterparts, but American institutions do offer students from rich and poor families alike the chance to realize their full potential. "America educates so many more people at university that one can't expect all those who go to be either as well informed or intelligent as the much narrower band who go to English universities," says Briton Christopher Ricks, professor of English at Boston University. Having instructed at Cambridge, Rick knows that teaching T. S. Eliot to British undergraduates is an easier task. Yet he finds teaching at B.U. very rewarding. "I'm not against elitism," he says, "but I happen to like having people who are more eager to learn."

The democratic impulse to reach out to so many first took seed after World War II, when the G.I. bill made funding for higher education available to all returning soldiers. As universities expanded to handle the sudden influx, they developed the flexibility that has become one of the hallmarks of American higher learning. "In the U.S. there is a system of infinite chances," says Diane Ravitch, assistant secretary of education. "At 35, you can decide to go back to college, upgrade your education, change your profession."

While Americans take such flexibility for granted, foreigners do not. To French students, who are commonly expected at age 16 to select both a university and a specific course of study, the American practice of jumping not only from department to department but also from school to school seems a luxury. Japanese students find it all but impossible to transfer credits from one school to another. Thus, students who initially enter a junior college and subsequently decide to earn a bachelor's degree must head overseas.

Many are attracted not only to the academic programs at a particular U.S. college but also to the larger community, which affords the chance to soak up the surrounding culture. Few foreign universities put much emphasis on the cozy communal life that characterizes American campuses from clubs and sports teams to student publications and theatrical societies. "The campus and the American university have become identical in people's minds," says Brown University President Vartan Gregorian. "In America it is assumed that a student's daily life is as important as his learning experience. . . ."

Foreign students also come in search of choices. America's menu of options—research universities, state institutions, private liberal-arts schools, community colleges, religious institutions, military academies—is unrivaled. "In Europe," says history professor Jonathan Steinberg, who has taught at both Harvard and Cambridge, "there is one system, and that is it." While students overseas usually must demonstrate expertise in a single field, whether law or philosophy or chemistry, most American universities insist that students sample natural and social sciences, languages and literature before choosing a field of concentration.

Such opposing philosophies grow out of different traditions and power structures. In Europe and Japan, universities are answerable only to a ministry of education, which sets academic standards and distributes money. While centralization ensures that all students are equipped with roughly the same resources and perform at roughly the same level, it also discourages experimentation. "When they make mistakes, they make big ones," says Robert Rosenzweig, president of the Association of American Universities. "They set a system in wrong directions, and it's like steering a supertanker."

U.S. colleges, on the other hand, are so responsive to cultural currents that they are often on the cutting edge of social change. Such sensitivity—some might argue hypersensitivity—to the culture around them reflects the broad array of constituencies to which college administrators must answer. The board of trustees, composed of community and national leaders, serves as a referee between the institutional culture and the surrounding community, alumni and corporate donors who often earmark monies for specific expenditures, student bodies that demand a voice in university life, legislators who apportion government funds, and an often feisty faculty.

Smaller colleges are particularly attractive to foreign students because they are likely to offer direct contact with professors. "We have one of the few systems in the world where students are actually expected to go to class," says Rosenzweig. With the exception of Britain, where much of the teaching takes place in one-on-one tutorials, European students rarely come into direct contact with professors until they reach graduate-level studies. Even lectures are optional in Europe, since students are graded solely on examinations, with no eye to class attendance or participation. . . .

In some respects, the independent spirit of the American university that foreigners admire comes down to dollars and cents. All U.S. colleges, private and public alike, must fight vigorously to stay alive. They compete not only for students but also for faculty and research grants. Such competition, though draining and distracting, can stimulate creativity and force administrators to remain attentive to student needs. "U.S. students pay for their education," says Ulrich Littmann, head of the German Fulbright Commission, "and demand a commensurate value for what they—or their parents—pay."

Most universities abroad have state funding, but that luxury has a steep price: universities have less opportunity to develop distinctive personalities and define their own missions. . . . If the financial crisis besetting U.S. campuses is mishandled, Americans may discover they don't know what they've got until it's gone.

A Fact-Finding Exercise

Read the passage again. Then read the following statements. Scan the article quickly to see if they are True (T) or False (F). If a statement is false, rewrite it so it is true.

1 _____ T _____ F   Most foreign students in American universities come from Canada.

_____

2 _____ T _____ F   Most U.S. high school graduates go to college.

_____

3 _____ T _____ F Foreign students attend U.S. universities only for educational reasons.

_____

4 _____ T _____ F Students in American universities must take a variety of courses in addition to courses in their major field.

_____

5 _____ T _____ F In an American university, it is not likely that students will be in direct contact with their teachers.

_____

6 _____ T _____ F Many American universities today are having financial problems.

_____

 B

Reading Analysis

Read each question carefully. Circle the number or letter of the correct answer, or write your answer in the space provided.

1 Read the first paragraph. What do college professors and administrators believe about American universities?

　a. American universities are superior to foreign universities.
　b. There is a financial crisis in American universities.
　c. They think that American universities are very expensive.

2 Read lines 14–15. "Asia led the way with 39,600 students from China and 36,610 from Japan, followed by India and Canada." This statement means

　a. Asian students arrived first
　b. Chinese students were in front of Japanese students
　c. more students came from Asia than from anywhere else
　d. Indian students followed Japanese students

3 Read lines 15–16. This statement means

    a. half of foreign students entered undergraduate school and half entered graduate school

    b. more foreign students entered undergraduate school than graduate school

4 Read lines 17–18. Which word is a synonym of **elite?**

_____

5 Read lines 18–21.

    a. **At some point in their life** means that most U.S. high school graduates

       1. enter college at the same age

       2. enter college before they get married

       3. enter college at different times

    b. What is the **comparable German population?**

       1. German high school graduates

       2. German college students

       3. German people

6 Read lines 21–23.

    a. What are the **Arbitur** and the **A levels?**

_____

    b. How do you know?

_____

7 Read lines 23–25.

    a. This statement means that

       1. European secondary training is more difficult than American secondary training

       2. American secondary training is more difficult than European secondary training

    b. **Secondary training** refers to

       1. graduate school

       2. college

       3. high school

8 Read lines 29–31.

   a. Counterparts refers to

      1. foreign college students
      2. American college students
      3. rich students
      4. poor students

   b. Rich and poor families alike means

      1. rich families are like poor families
      2. both rich families *and* poor families
      3. rich families and poor families like each other

9 Read lines 43–44. **Chances** means

   a. risks
   b. opportunities
   c. accidents

10 Read lines 46–49. **Jumping from department to department** means

   a. taking gymnastics classes
   b. changing universities
   c. changing majors

11 Read lines 50–52.

   a. all but impossible means

      1. completely impossible
      2. almost impossible
      3. everything is impossible

   b. Thus means

      1. afterwards
      2. in addition
      3. as a result

   c. Initially means

      1. first
      2. second
      3. third

d. Subsequently means

   1. first
   2. next
   3. last

12 Read lines 61–63.

   a. Which word is a synonym of **choices?**

   _____

   b. What is between the dashes (—)?
   1. New information about options
   2. Examples of options
   3. Contrasting information

13 Read lines 87–93.

   a. This statement means that students in European classes
   1. never attend classes
   2. must attend classes
   3. do not have to attend classes

   b. Optional means
   1. necessary
   2. not necessary
   3. important

14 Read lines 102–104. What follows the colon (:)?

   a. The cost of state funding
   b. An explanation of the price
   c. A description of universities

15 In lines 16, 60, and elsewhere there are ellipses (. . .) at the end of the paragraph. These dots indicate that

   a. the last sentence is incomplete
   b. text has been omitted from the article
   c. there are exactly three sentences missing

Information Organization

Read the article again. Underline what you think are the main ideas. Then scan the article and complete the following chart, using the sentences that you have underlined to help you. You will use this chart later to answer specific questions about the article. Not all the boxes will be filled in.

	United States	Japan	Europe
Percent of high school graduates who attend college			
Differences between universities (freedom of choice)	1. 2. 3.		France:
Differences in types of colleges			
Funding for education			

D Information Organization
Quiz and Summary

Read each question carefully. Use your notes to answer the questions.
Do not refer back to the text. When you are finished, write a brief summary
of the article.

1 **a.** What percent of U.S. high school graduates enter college?

_____

b. What percent of high school graduates enter college in countries
in Europe and Asia?

_____

_____

2 What are some differences between universities in the United States and
those in Europe and in Asia?

_____

_____

_____

3 How are colleges in the United States different financially from colleges
in other countries?

_____

_____

_____

Summary

_____

_____

_____

_____

_____

_____

Dictionary Skills

Read the dictionary entry for each word. Then look at how the word is used in the sentence. Write the number of the correct definition and the synonym or meaning in the space provided. Remember that you may need to change the wording of the definition in order to have a grammatically correct sentence.

1 | **roughly** *adv* **1** : in a rough manner : as **a** : with harshness or violence **b** : in crude fashion : imperfectly **2** : without completeness or exactness : approximately

Many of the foreigners entered graduate and undergraduate programs

in ( ) _____ equal numbers.

2 | **match** *v* **1** **a** : to encounter successfully as an antagonist **b** *(1)* : to set in competition or opposition *(2)* : to provide with a worthy competitor **c** : to set in comparison **2** : to join or give in marriage **3** **a** *(1)* : to put in a set possessing equal or harmonizing attributes *(2)* : to cause to correspond : suit **b** *(1)* : to be the counterpart of; *also* : to compare favorably with *(2)* : to harmonize with **c** : to provide with a counterpart **d** : to provide funds complementary . . .

Not all U.S. collegians can ( ) _____ the

performance of their foreign counterparts.

3 | **practice** *n* **1** **a** : actual performance or application **b** : a repeated or customary action **c** : the usual way of doing something **d** : the form, manner, and order of conducting legal suits and prosecutions **2** **a** : systematic exercise for proficiency **b** : the condition of being proficient through systematic exercise . . .

The American ( ) _____ of jumping from

department to department seems a luxury.

4 | **demonstrate** *v* **1** : to show clearly **2** **a** : to prove or make clear by reasoning or evidence **b** : to illustrate and explain *esp* with many examples **3** : to show or prove the value or efficiency of to a prospective buyer

Students overseas must ( ) _____ expertise in a

single field, whether law or philosophy or chemistry.

By permission. From *Merriam-Webster's Collegiate® Dictionary*, 11th Edition © 2010 by Merriam-Webster, Incorporated (www.Merriam-Webster.com).

F Word Forms

PART 1

In English, some adjectives become nouns by adding the suffix *-ity*, for example, *fatal (adj.), fatality (n.)*.

Complete each sentence with the correct form of the words on the left. **Use the singular or plural form of the nouns.**

individual *(adj.)*

individuality *(n.)*

1   Even though they may be in a large class, students like to receive _____ treatment from their teachers. Everyone likes to preserve their _____ even if they are part of a large group.

creative *(adj.)*

creativity *(n.)*

2   People can demonstrate _____ in many ways. For instance, some people have _____ ways of expressing themselves in words, others in decorating their homes, and still others in painting or photography.

diverse *(adj.)*

diversity *(n.)*

3   In a typical ESL classroom, you will find students from a wide _____ of countries. In fact, even if students are from the same country, they may come from _____ backgrounds.

national *(adj.)*

nationality *(n.)*

4   Each country has its own _____ anthem, or song. There are students of very different _____ in this class.

flexible (adj.)

flexibility (n.)

⑤ There is considerable _____ in this English program. For example, the days and the hours of classes are quite _____ .

In English, some adjectives become nouns by deleting the final -t and adding -ce, for example, *negligent (adj.), negligence (n.).*
   Complete each sentence with the correct form of the words on the left.

excellent (adj.)

excellence (n.)

① We all strive for _____ , and sometimes we achieve it. Even if everything we do isn't always _____ , we can always try harder the next time.

different (adj.)

difference (n.)

② I haven't noticed any _____ in the quality of the food in this restaurant since they hired a new cook last week. The meals don't taste any _____ than they did last week.

dominant (adj.)

dominance (n.)

③ According to geneticists, brown eyes are always _____ over blue eyes. This _____ means that if one parent has brown eyes and the other parent has blue eyes, the children will most likely have brown eyes.

independent *(adj.)*

independence *(n.)*

4　In the past several years, many countries have struggled for and gained their _____ .
These newly _____ countries usually have to contend with many difficulties as they try to maintain stability.

important *(adj.)*

importance *(n.)*

5　The students want to know how much _____ the teacher is going to give to their homework. In other words, they want to know how _____ the homework is to their grade.

Word Partnership	Use *independence* with:
adj.	**economic/financial** independence
v.	**fight for** independence, **gain** independence
n.	**a struggle for** independence

Word Partnership	Use *importance* with:
adj.	**critical** importance, **enormous** importance, **growing/increasing** importance, **utmost** importance
v.	**place less/more** importance **on** *something*, **recognize the** importance, **understand the** importance
n.	**self**-importance, **sense of** importance

Critical Thinking Strategies

Read each question carefully, and write a response. Remember that there is no one correct answer. Your response depends on what **you** think.

1 In lines 59–60, Brown University President Gregorian says, "In America it is assumed that a student's daily life is as important as his learning experience." From this statement, what expectations, other than academic, can we assume that American universities have of all their students, including foreign students?

_____

_____

_____

2 Read lines 65–68. Why do you think American universities have these requirements?

_____

_____

_____

3 In lines 94–101, the author discusses the money factor. What connection does she make between paying for one's education and the university's responsibility to its students?

_____

_____

_____

4 Read lines 102–104. What do you think the author believes is the effect of state funding on foreign universities?

_____

_____

_____

5 Think about how the author presented the information in this article.

    a. Do you think she was objective or subjective in describing the American university system? Why do you think so? Refer to specific sentences in the reading to support your opinion.

_____

_____

_____

    b. Do you think she was objective or subjective in describing foreign students? Why do you think so? Refer to specific sentences in the reading to support your opinion.

_____

_____

_____

H Topics for Discussion and Writing

1 Describe your experience as a foreign student in the United States, or the experience of someone you know who has studied in the United States. What was positive about the experience? What was negative about the experience? Explain.

2 Work with one or two partners. List the potential difficulties of being a foreign student in the United States. Discuss how you can deal with these problems to reduce or eliminate them.

3 One problem that foreign students frequently encounter is loneliness and difficulty making friends. Work with a partner. Plan several strategies for reducing loneliness and making friends.

4 **Write in your journal.** Imagine that a friend wants to come to the United States to study. Write your friend a letter. Tell him or her what to expect as a foreign student and how to prepare before leaving home.

Follow-Up Activities

1 Refer back to the chart in Exercise C on page 167. Choose two differences between American universities and foreign universities. Using the following chart, write the differences you have chosen and list what you think the advantages and disadvantages are. Compare your chart with your classmates' charts.

	In the United States	In Japan	In Europe
Difference 1			
Advantages			
Disadvantages			
Difference 2			
Advantages			
Disadvantages			

2 **a.** Refer to the College Survey below. The purpose of the survey is to collect data regarding students' reasons for studying in a foreign country. As a class, add more reasons to #4.

b. Work alone or with a partner. Go outside and survey two or three international students. Then bring back your data and combine it with the other students' information. How do your results compare with the results you obtained in your class? Do international students have similar reasons for studying in another country? What are the main reasons you discovered, in both your in-class and out-of-class surveys?

COLLEGE SURVEY			
Informant's Gender	**M / F**	**M / F**	**M / F**
1. What country are you from?			
2. What field do you plan to major in?			
3. Are you going to enter an undergraduate program or a graduate program?			
4. Why did you choose to study in the United States? Please indicate all the reasons that apply to you. • the cost of education • to study my major • the choice of courses • to improve my English • to get away from home • to learn about another country • other reasons (please specify) • _____ • _____ • _____			
5. Put the reasons you have indicated for studying in the United States in order of importance. That is, write **1** next to your most important reason, **2** next to your second most important reason, etc.			

Cloze Quiz

J

Complete the passage with words from the list. Use each word only once.

attracted	emphasis	flooded	practice
campuses	envy	followed	provide
colleges	equal	foreigners	students
community	expected	impossible	troubles
countries	flexibility	initially	undergraduate

If sheer numbers _____ (1) any proof, America's universities

and _____ (2) are the _____ (3) of the world.

For all their abiding _____ (4), the United States' 3,500

institutions were _____ (5) with 407,530 students from 193

different _____ (6) last year. Asia led the way with 39,600

_____ (7) from China and 36,610 from Japan, _____ (8)

by India and Canada. Many of the _____ (9) entered graduate and

_____ (10) programs in roughly _____ (11) numbers. . . .

Americans take academic _____ (12) for granted, but foreigners

do not. To French students, who are commonly _____ (13) at age

16 to select both a university and a specific course of study, the American

_____ (14) of jumping not only from department to department

but also from school to school seems a luxury. Japanese students find it all

but _____ (15) to transfer credits from one school to another. Thus,

students who _____ (16) enter a junior college and subsequently

decide to earn a bachelor's degree must head overseas.

Many are _____ not only to the academic programs
(17)
at a particular U.S. college but also to the larger _____ ,
(18)
which affords the chance to soak up the surrounding culture. Few foreign
universities put much _____ on the cozy communal life that
(19)
characterizes American _____ : from clubs and sports teams
(20)
to student publications and theatrical societies.

UNIT 3 | REVIEW

Crossword Puzzle

Read the clues on the next page. Write the answers in the correct spaces
in the puzzle.

Crossword Puzzle Clues

3. To say what will happen before it occurs
6. The opposite of **first**
8. John is going to _____ a problem. After he presents it, we will try to solve it.
9. A problem with no perfect solution
11. Guess too low
14. A _____ is one possible form of government.
15. A cat is a very _____ animal. It wants to know everything.
17. The study of the parts of the body
18. The opposite of **less**
19. Please turn _____ the lights. I am going to sleep.
21. Privileged
22. The past tense of **get**
23. The system of checks and _____ ensures that no one in government has too much power.
26. When something is _____ , it is a choice; it is not necessary.

1. Changeable
2. International students must _____ their English proficiency before being admitted to an American college or university.
4. The past of **do**
5. Thinking
7. First
8. A customary or often repeated action
10. High quality; superiority
12. He feels inferior. He feels like a _____ citizen.
13. Congress is called the _____ branch of government because its purpose is to make laws.
14. Dissatisfaction
16. Approximately
18. A _____ consists of more than half (at least 50%) of a group.
20. Speak informally
24. Each; every
25. Girl, _____ , woman, man

Discussion

1. In some countries, the government pays all educational costs for students. In other countries, it is the responsibility of each family. Each system has its advantages and disadvantages. Who do you think should cover the costs of education? In your response, discuss the advantages and disadvantages of both systems.

2. In some countries, the government sets up rules and guidelines that affect people's lives in many areas, e.g., family size, education, employment, retirement. Work in a small group. Choose one of these areas, or another area of your choice. The government has chosen your committee to set up guidelines for this area. In your group, make a list of rules. Present your rules to the class, and give reasons for your decisions.

Science and Technology

Antarctica: Whose Continent Is It Anyway?

by Daniel and Sally Grotta, *Popular Science*

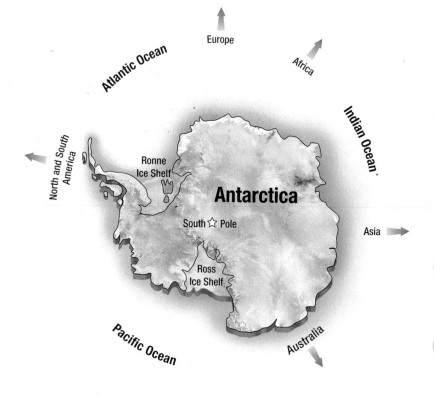

Prereading Preparation

1. Where is Antarctica?

2. With a partner, discuss what you know about Antarctica, and fill in the chart below with your information.

3. Some scientists study Antarctica. What are possible reasons why?

4. Look at the title. What do you think this article will discuss?

Climate	Geography	People	Animals	Plants

Track 10

Antarctica: Whose Continent Is It Anyway?

Handwritten margin notes (left):
Antarctica extends unbroken along the Ross sea for hundreds of miles

The coldest Place on Earth

① scientists.
② tourists.
③ environmentalists.
④ preseving Antarctica as a kind of world park will deprive the rest of The world of much needed oil and mineral reserves.

*Antarctica unique attributes it is the coldest, driest, and highest continent

*The Scientists estimate That 70% of The world's fresh water is locked away in Antarctica ice cap.

Handwritten margin notes (right):
The white ice cliff higher Than The ship's mast

subject of conflicting interests

2 The scientists Treasure The unparalleled advantages for Research

Antarctica is vital to life on Earth

Last February, the *World Discoverer*, our cruise ship, stopped in front of a white ice cliff higher than the ship's mast. As large as France, the Ross Ice Shelf of Antarctica extends unbroken along the Ross Sea for hundreds of miles.

Like other passengers on our cruise ship, we had been lured by an irresistible attraction: the chance to visit the most remote place on Earth, and the most unusual. The coldest place on Earth is also the subject of conflicting interests: scientists, tourists, environmentalists, oil and mineral seekers. Scientists treasure the unparalleled advantages for research; tourists prize the chance to visit Earth's last frontier; environmentalists fear that increases in both activities will pollute the continent and jeopardize its fabulous creatures; others contend that preserving Antarctica as a kind of world park will deprive the rest of the world of much needed oil and mineral reserves.

Fears of Antarctica's ruin through commercial exploitation have been partly reduced by the October, 1991, 31-nation signing of the Madrid Protocol, which bans oil and gas exploration for the next 50 years. But Antarctica's unique attributes—it is the coldest, driest, and highest continent—will keep it at the focus of conflicting scientific and touristic interests.

Think of a place as remote as the far side of the moon, as strange as Saturn and as inhospitable as Mars, and that will give some idea of what Antarctica is like. A mere 2.4 percent of its 5.4 million-square-mile land mass is ice-free, and then, only for a few months a year. Scientists estimate that 70 percent of the world's fresh water is locked away in Antarctica's icecap; if it were ever to melt, sea levels might rise 200 feet. In Antarctica, winds can blow at better than 200 mph, and temperatures drop as low as minus 128.6°F. There's not a single village or town, not a tree, bush, or blade of grass on the entire continent.

But far from being merely a useless continent, Antarctica is vital to life on Earth. The continent's vast ice fields reflect sunlight back into space, preventing the planet from overheating. The cold water that the breakaway icebergs generate flows north and mixes with equatorial warm water, producing currents, clouds, and ultimately creating complex weather patterns. Antarctic seas teem with life, making them an important link in the world food chain. The frigid waters of the Southern Ocean are home to species of birds and mammals that are found nowhere else.

5

10

15

20

25

30

183

The National Science Foundation (NSF) is the government agency responsible for the U.S. stations in Antarctica. Because of the continent's extreme cold and almost complete isolation, the NSF considers it to be the best place to study and understand such phenomena as temperature circulation in the oceans, unique animal life, ozone depletion, and glacial history. And buried deep in layers of Antarctic ice lie clues to ancient climates, clues such as trapped bubbles of atmospheric gases, which can help predict whether present and future global warming poses a real threat.

Until scientists began the first serious study of the continent during the 1957–58 International Geophysical Year (IGY), a multicountry cooperative research project, Antarctica was dismissed as a vast, useless continent.

Based upon early explorations and questionable land grants, seven countries, including Great Britain, Chile, and Argentina, claim sovereignty over vast tracts of the continent. However, as IGY wound down, the question of who owns Antarctica came to a head. The 12 participating countries reached an international agreement, the Antarctic Treaty, which took effect in June 1961. The number has since grown, making 39 in all. It established Antarctica as a "continent for science and peace," and temporarily set aside all claims of sovereignty for as long as the treaty remains in effect.

The rules of the treaty meant that as tourists to Antarctica, passengers on our cruise ship needed neither passports nor visas. Except for a handful of sites of special scientific interest, specially protected areas, and specially managed areas, there was nothing to restrict us from wandering anywhere we wanted.

Primarily because of its scientific and ecological importance, many scientists feel that Antarctica should be dedicated to research only. They feel that tourists should not be permitted to come. However, recent events have shown that the greatest future threat to Antarctica may not be tourism or scientific stations, but the worldwide thirst for oil and minerals. "The reason the Antarctic Treaty was negotiated and went through so quickly," geologist John Splettstoesser explains, "is that at the time, relatively few minerals were known to exist there."

By the early 1970s, however, there were some indications that there might be gas and oil in Antarctica. The treaty countries decided that no commercial companies would be permitted to explore for resources. The Madrid Protocol bans all exploration or commercial exploitation of natural resources on the continent for the next 50 years.

Like the Antarctic Treaty itself, the Madrid Protocol is binding only on the 39 treaty countries. There's nothing to stop non-treaty countries from establishing commercial bases anywhere on the continent and doing whatever they please.

Where do we go from here? So far, no non-treaty nation has expressed a serious interest in setting up for business in Antarctica. So far, none of the countries claiming sovereignty has moved to formally annex Antarctic territory.

So whose continent is Antarctica, anyway? Former Vice President Albert Gore best expresses the feelings of those of us who have fallen in love with this strange and spectacular land: "I think that it should be held in trust as a global ecological reserve for all the people of the world, not just in this generation, but later generations to come as well."

 Fact-Finding Exercise

Read the passage again. Then read the following statements. Scan the article quickly to see if they are True (T) or False (F). If a statement is false, rewrite it so that it is true.

1 _____ T ___✓___ F   Most people agree that Antarctica should be used for research.

_____

2 ____✓ T _____ F   Antarctica is the coldest place on Earth.

3 ____✓ T _____ F   Most of Antarctica is ice-free.

4 ____✓ T _____ F   Antarctica is a useless continent.

5 ____✓ T _____ F   Important information about the past may be buried under the Antarctic ice.

6 ____✓ T _____ F   Thirty-nine countries have agreed to the Antarctic Treaty.

7 _____ T _____ F   Most tourists feel that Antarctica should be dedicated to scientific research only.

8 _____ T _____ F   The Madrid Protocol allows countries to explore Antarctica for natural resources.

B

Reading Analysis

Read each question carefully. Circle the number or letter of the correct answer, or write your answer in the space provided.

1 **a.** Read lines 1–2. What is the ***World Discoverer?***

The Ross Ice Shelf of Antarcticta

   b. Who does **our** refer to?

_____

2 Read lines 2–3. What is as large as France?

   a. The *World Discoverer*
   b. The Ross Ice Shelf
   c. Antarctica

3 Read lines 4–6.

   a. **Lure** means

     1. invite
     2. visit
     3. attract

   b. What is **an irresistible attraction?**

_____

_____

   c. What follows the **colon (:)?**

     1. Additional information
     2. An example
     3. An explanation

4 In lines 6–7, what is the coldest place on Earth?

_____

5 Read lines 8–12. In line 10, who does **others** refer to?

   a. Tourists
   b. Scientists
   c. Environmentalists
   d. Oil and mineral seekers

CHAPTER 10   ANTARCTICA: WHOSE CONTINENT IS IT ANYWAY?   187

6 In lines 20–21, what does **a mere 2.4 percent** mean?

   a. only 2.4 percent

   b. exactly 2.4 percent

   c. approximately 2.4 percent

7 Read lines 30–31. Which one of the following examples represents a **food chain?**

   a. orange tree → oranges → people

   b. insects → birds → cats

   c. Farmer → supermarket → people

8 Read lines 42–44.

   a. What is **IGY?**

   _____

   b. When was Antarctica thought of as a useless continent?

     1. Before IGY

     2. After IGY

   c. When did scientists begin the first serious study of Antarctica?

     1. Before 1957

     2. 1957–1958

     3. After 1958

9 Read lines 47–48. "As IGY wound down, the question of who owns Antarctica came to a head." What does **came to a head** mean?

   a. Started a big argument

   b. Grew to a large size

   c. Became very important

10 In line 52, what does **sovereignty** mean?

   a. Ownership

   b. Boundaries

   c. Continent

11 In line 54, what is **a handful?**

    a. A small number

    b. A large number

12 Read lines 54–56. Which word is a synonym for **sites?**

_____

13 In lines 61–63, when does **at the time** refer to?

_____

14 In line 70, what are **non-treaty countries?**

_____

15 a. In lines 72–74, what does **so far** mean?

      1. In the future

      2. Up to now

      3. Never

    b. Why do the authors write **so far** twice in the same paragraph?

      1. For repetition

      2. For contrast

      3. For emphasis

16 Read lines 73–74, "So far none of the countries claiming sovereignty has moved to formally annex Antarctic territory." This sentence means that none of the countries claiming sovereignty

    a. has moved to make Antarctica part of its own country

    b. has moved to set up a government in Antarctica

    c. has sent a number of people to settle in Antarctica

17 Read the last paragraph. Who thinks this way about Antarctica?

    a. Only Albert Gore

    b. The authors

    c. Everyone who loves Antarctica

Information Organization

Read the article again. Underline what you think are the main ideas. Then scan the article and complete the following outline, using the sentences that you have underlined to help you. You will use this outline later to answer specific questions about the article.

I. People with Conflicting Interests in Antarctica

    A. _____

        Reason: _____

    B. Tourists _____

        Reason: *They prize the chance to visit Earth's last frontier*

    C. _____

        Reason: _____

    D. _____

        Reason: _____

II. The Madrid Protocol

    A. Date: _____

    B. Original number of participating nations: _____

    C. Purpose: _____

III. _____

    A. _____

    B. _____

    C. *Winds blow at more than 200 mph*

    D. _____

    E. *There are no villages, towns, or plants*

IV. Antarctica Is Vital to Life on Earth

    A. _____

    B. _____

    C. _____

    D. _____

V. The Antarctic Treaty's Purpose

    A. _____

    B. _____

    C. _____

D

Information Organization
Quiz and Summary

Read each question carefully. Use your notes to answer the questions. Do not refer back to the text. When you are finished, write a brief summary of the article.

1 Why are there conflicting interests regarding Antarctica?

_____

_____

2 What is the Madrid Protocol?

_____

_____

3 Describe the continent of Antarctica.

_____

_____

4 Is Antarctica necessary to life on Earth? Why, or why not?

_____

_____

5 What is the purpose of the Antarctic Treaty?

_____

_____

Summary

_____

_____

_____

_____

_____

_____

Dictionary Skills

Read the dictionary entry for each word. Then look at how the word is used in the sentence. Write the number of the correct definition and the synonym or meaning in the space provided. Remember that you may need to change the wording of the definition in order to have a grammatically correct sentence.

1 **remote** _adj_ **1** : separated by an interval or space greater than usual **2** : far removed in space, time, or relation : divergent **3** : out-of-the-way, secluded **4** : acting, acted on, or controlled indirectly or from a distance; _also_ : relating to the acquisition of information about a distant object (as by radar or photography) without coming into physical contact with it . . .

Think of a place as (   ) _____ as the far side of the moon.

By permission. From _Merriam-Webster's Collegiate® Dictionary_, 11th Edition © 2010 by Merriam-Webster, Incorporated (www.Merriam-Webster.com).

2 | **contend** *v* **1** : to strive or vie in contest or rivalry or against difficulties : struggle **2** : to strive in debate : argue

Some people (   ) _____ that preserving Antarctica as a kind of world park will deprive the rest of the world of oil and mineral reserves.

3 | **dismiss** *v* **1** : to permit or cause to leave **2** : to remove from position or service : discharge **3** **a** : to reject serious consideration of **b** : to put out of judicial consideration

Until scientists began the first serious study of Antarctica in 1957, most people (   ) _____ the continent. They considered it a vast, useless place.

Word Forms

PART 1

In English, many verbs become nouns by adding the suffix *-ion* or *-tion*, for example, *suggest (v.), suggestion (n.).*

Complete each sentence with the correct form of the words on the left. **Use the correct tense of the verbs, in either the affirmative or the negative form. Use the singular or plural form of the nouns.**

reflect *(v.)*

reflection *(n.)*

1 The baby saw her _____ in the mirror and smiled. She didn't understand that the mirror actually _____ her own image, not another child's.

reduce *(v.)*

reduction *(n.)*

2 Neil _____ the amount of food he eats because he has gone on a diet. He is working on a weight _____ of ten to fifteen pounds in a month.

By permission. From *Merriam-Webster's Collegiate® Dictionary*, 11th Edition © 2010 by Merriam-Webster, Incorporated (www.Merriam-Webster.com).

deplete *(v.)*

depletion *(n.)*

3   We _____ the world's supply of oil and natural gas at a steady rate. In order to reduce the rate of _____ of these natural resources, we need to resort to alternate sources of energy.

exploit *(v.)*

exploitation *(n.)*

4   If we _____ our natural resources wisely, and take care to protect the environment, we will have a supply of oil and gas for a long time. However, it is very easy for unwise _____ to leave the Earth both polluted and without resources.

negotiate *(v.)*

negotiation *(n.)*

5   The two computer firms entered into serious _____ in order to merge their companies into one. They not only _____ acceptable terms, but also decided where to relocate the newly formed company.

PART 2

In English, many verbs become nouns by adding the suffix -*ment,* for example, *improve (v.), improvement (n.).*

     Complete each sentence with the correct form of the words on the left. **Use the correct tense of the verbs, in either the affirmative or the negative form. Use the singular or plural form of the nouns.**

employ *(v.)*

employment *(n.)*

1   In the past, many companies had very unfair _____ practices. For example, they _____ anyone they were prejudiced against, and they often made people work six or even seven days a week.

equip *(v.)*

equipment *(n.)*

2   The manager of Fielder's Choice always _____ the high school baseball team.

He provides the team with all the basic

_____ it needs in return for having his

shop's name on the team's uniforms.

govern *(v.)*   ③   I'm going to vote for Joan Harrington for mayor because

government *(n.)*   I think that our city _____ needs a change.

I really believe that Joan _____ the city

much better than the present mayor has been doing.

manage *(v.)*   ④   Bill and Carla _____ the new company

management *(n.)*   together beginning next year. The board of directors

believes that the new _____ will help the

company improve its productivity over the next

five years.

establish *(v.)*   ⑤   The government recently _____ an

establishment *(n.)*   agency to investigate reports of environmental

pollution. Many private environmental groups praised

the government for its timely _____ of

this agency.

Word Partnership	Use *management* with:
n.	**business** management, **crisis** management, management **skills**, management **style** **waste** management management **team,** management **training**
adj.	**new** management, **senior** management

Word Partnership	Use *establish* with:
n.	establish **control,** establish **independence,** establish **rules** establish **contact,** establish **relations,** establish *someone's* **identity**

Critical Thinking Strategies

Read each question carefully, and write a response. Remember that there is no one correct answer. Your response depends on what **you** think.

1 Read lines 21–23. What do you think would happen if sea levels rose 200 feet?

_____

_____

_____

_____

2 Read lines 38–41. What do you think are some other reasons that it may be important to study ancient climates?

_____

_____

_____

_____

3 Read lines 59–63. When the Antarctic Treaty was signed in 1961, very little was known about the continent's natural resources. According to John Splettstoesser, what is the relationship between the quick signing of the treaty and the lack of information about the resources?

_____

_____

_____

_____

Topics for Discussion and Writing

H

1. The authors ask who Antarctica belongs to. Whose continent *is* Antarctica? Do you think it should belong to one country, many countries, or to no one? Write a composition explaining your opinion.

2. **Write in your journal.** Reread the fifth paragraph (lines 18–25). In this paragraph, the authors describe Antarctica by comparing it with other places and by giving facts about it. The authors are trying to convey an image and a feeling about this unusual continent. Imagine that you are visiting Antarctica. Write a journal entry in which you describe what you see and how being in Antarctica makes you feel. Do you have feelings similar to those of the first explorers?

Follow-Up Activities

I

1. Scientists, tourists, environmentalists, and oil and mineral seekers all have different opinions about what to do with Antarctica. Choose one of these four groups, and imagine that you are a member. Working with a partner or in a small group, make a list of reasons why Antarctica is important to your particular group. Compare your list with your classmates' lists. Then as a class, decide which group has the strongest reasons to support its point of view.

2. Form a panel of experts. Write a set of guidelines for the protection and use of Antarctica by all the interested countries of the world. You want to be fair to all the interested countries. You also want to try to satisfy the four groups previously mentioned: scientists, environmentalists, tourists, and oil and mineral seekers.

3. In the third paragraph (lines 8–12), the authors say that tourists consider Antarctica to be Earth's last frontier. However, other people do not agree with this statement. They believe that there are other places on Earth that have not yet been fully explored and that are still exciting, challenging places to go to. Alone, or with a partner, decide what other such places exist on Earth and examine why people would be interested in going there.

J Cloze Quiz

Complete the passage with words from the list. Use each word only once.

agreement	continent	however	research
all	countries	long	science
Antarctica	effect	number	scientists
Argentina	established	question	temporarily
claims	explorations	remains	useless

Until _____ (1) began the first serious study of the _____ (2) during the 1957–58 International Geophysical Year (IGY), a multicountry cooperative _____ (3) project, Antarctica was dismissed as a vast, _____ (4) continent.

Based upon early _____ (5) and questionable land grants, seven _____ (6), including Great Britain, Chile, and _____ (7), claim sovereignty over vast tracts of the continent. _____ (8), as IGY wound down, the _____ (9) of who owns _____ (10) came to a head. The 12 participating countries reached an international _____ (11), the Antarctic Treaty, which took _____ (12) in June 1961. The _____ (13) has since grown, making 39 in _____ (14). It _____ (15) Antarctica as a "continent for _____ (16) and peace," and _____ (17) set aside all _____ (18) of sovereignty for as _____ (19) as the treaty _____ (20) in effect.

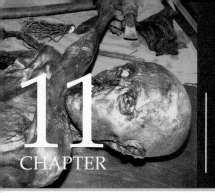

11 CHAPTER | A Messenger from the Past

by James Shreeve
Discover

Prereading Preparation

1. Do you think it's important to learn about humans of the past? Why, or why not?

2. What are some ways we can learn about humans of the past?

3. Read the title of this article and look at the picture. Who is the messenger from the past? What message, or information, can he give us today?

A Messenger from the Past

1   His people said good-bye and watched him walk off toward the mountains. They had little reason to fear for his safety: the man was well dressed in insulated clothing and equipped with tools needed to survive the Alpine climate. However, as weeks passed without his return, they must have grown

5   worried, then anxious, and finally resigned. After many years everyone who knew him had died, and not even a memory of the man remained.

   Then, on an improbably distant day, he came down from the mountain. Things had changed a bit: it wasn't the Bronze Age anymore, and he was a celebrity.

   When a melting glacier released its hold on a 4,000-year-old corpse in

10   September, it was quite rightly called one of the most important archeological finds of the century. Discovered by a German couple hiking at 10,500 feet in the Italian Tyrol near the Austrian border, the partially freeze-dried body still wore remnants of leather garments and boots that had been stuffed with straw for insulation. The hikers alerted scientists from the University of Innsbruck in

15   Austria, whose more complete examination revealed that the man was tattooed on his back and behind his knee. At his side was a bronze ax of a type typical in southern central Europe around 2000 B.C. On his expedition—perhaps to hunt or to search for metal ore—he had also carried an all-purpose stone knife, a wooden backpack, a bow and a quiver, a small bag containing a flint lighter and

20   kindling, and an arrow repair kit in a leather pouch.

   Such everyday gear gives an unprecedented perspective on life in early Bronze Age Europe. "The most exciting thing is that we genuinely appear to be looking at a man who had some kind of accident in the course of a perfectly ordinary trip," says archeologist Ian Kinnes of the British Museum. "These are

25   not artifacts placed in a grave, but the fellow's own possessions."

   Unlike the Egyptians and Mesopotamians of the time, who had more advanced civilizations with cities and central authority, the Ice Man and his countrymen lived in a society built around small, stable villages. He probably spoke in a tongue ancestral to current European languages. Furthermore, though

30   he was a member of a farming culture, he may well have been hunting when he died, to add meat to his family's diet. X-rays of the quiver showed that it contained 14 arrows. While his backpack was empty, careful exploration of the trench where he died revealed remnants of animal skin and bones at the same spot where the pack lay. There was also the remainder of a pile of berries.

35   Clearly the man didn't starve to death.

   So why did the Ice Man die? The trench provided him with shelter from the elements, and he also had a braided mat of grass to keep him warm. If injury or illness caused the Ice Man's death, an autopsy on the 4,000-year-old victim could turn up some clues. The circumstances of his death may have preserved such evidence, as well as other details of his life. Freeze-dried by the frigid climate, his inner organs and other soft tissues are much better preserved than those of dried-up Egyptian mummies or the waterlogged Scandinavian "Bog Men" found in recent years.

One concern, voiced by archeologist Colin Renfrew of Cambridge University, is that the hot TV lights that greeted the hunter's return to civilization may have damaged these fragile tissues, jeopardizing a chance to recover additional precious genetic information from his chromosomes. If not, Renfrew says, "it may be possible to get very long DNA sequences out of this material. This is far and away the most exciting aspect of the discovery."

For the time being, all biological research has literally been put on ice at the University of Innsbruck while an international team of experts, led by researcher Konrad Spindler, puzzles out a way to thaw the body without destroying it. As sensational as it sounds, it remains to be seen how useful 4,000-year-old human DNA will really be. "The problem is that we are dealing with a single individual," says evolutionary biologist Robert Sokal of the State University of New York at Stony Brook. "In order to make statements about the population that existed at the time, we need more specimens."

The wish for more messengers from the past may yet come true. Five more bodies of mountain climbers, all of whom died within the past 50 years, have emerged from melting Austrian mountain ice this summer. The Ice Man's return from the Tyrol has demonstrated that the local climate is warmer now than it has been for 4,000 years. People are beginning to wonder—and plan for—what the melting ice may reveal next.

"No one ever thought this could happen," says Christopher Stringer, an anthropologist at the Natural History Museum in London. "The fact that it has occurred once means that people will now be looking for it again."

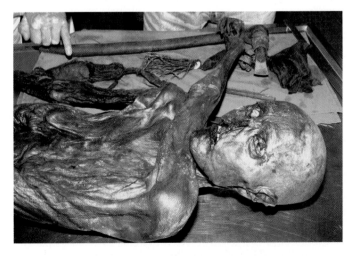

Fact-Finding Exercise

Read the passage once. Then read the following statements. Scan the article quickly to see if they are True (T) or False (F). If a statement is false, rewrite it so that it is true.

1 _____ T _____ F   The Ice Man lived 4,000 years ago.

_____

2 _____ T _____ F   The Ice Man was discovered in Europe by scientists.

_____

3 _____ T _____ F   Scientists aren't sure how the Ice Man died.

_____

4 _____ T _____ F   The Ice Man's body had been frozen for 4,000 years.

_____

5 _____ T _____ F   Scientists have examined the Ice Man to get genetic information.

_____

6 _____ T _____ F   More bodies of mountain climbers who died 4,000 years ago were discovered.

_____

Reading Analysis

Read each question carefully. Circle the number or letter of the correct answer, or write your answer in the space provided.

1 Read line 7. This statement means

   a. the Ice Man walked down from the mountain
   b. the Ice Man woke up on the mountain
   c. the Ice Man's body was brought down from the mountain

2 In line 9, what does the **4,000-year-old corpse** refer to?

_____

3 Read lines 14–16. **Whose** refers to

   a. the Ice Man
   b. the scientists
   c. the hikers

4 Read lines 17–22.
   a. What are some examples of the Ice Man's **everyday gear?**

_____

   b. **Gear** means

   1. clothes
   2. equipment
   3. weapons

5 Read lines 28–29. In this sentence, what does **tongue** refer to?

   a. The Ice Man's mouth
   b. The Ice Man's accent
   c. The Ice Man's language

6 In line 29, what follows **furthermore?**

   a. An example
   b. A theory
   c. Additional information

7 Read line 35. What does **clearly** mean?

   a. Unfortunately
   b. Obviously
   c. Possibly

8 Read lines 39–40.

   a. What does **evidence** mean?

     1. Proof of how the Ice Man died
     2. Clues to how the Ice Man died
     3. Theories describing how the Ice Man may have died

   b. What does **as well as** mean?

     1. Better than
     2. As good as
     3. In addition to

9 Read lines 40–42. What are the Ice Man's **inner organs and other soft tissues?**

   a. Parts of his body
   b. Objects he had with him
   c. The food remaining in his stomach

10 In lines 47–48, **far and away** indicates

   a. distance
   b. importance
   c. excitement

11 Read lines 49–51.

   a. For the time being means

     1. for a long time
     2. for now
     3. for a human being

   b. Thaw means

     1. melt, as ice becomes water
     2. bring back to life
     3. bring back to normal temperature

12 In line 57, **yet** means

   a. still
   b. but
   c. not

13 Read lines 64–65. What does **it** refer to?

_____

_____

Information Organization

Read the article again. Underline what you think are the main ideas. Then scan the article and complete the flowchart, using the sentences that you have underlined to help you. For each possible cause of death, circle *yes, no,* or *maybe*, based on your reasoning from the information in the text.

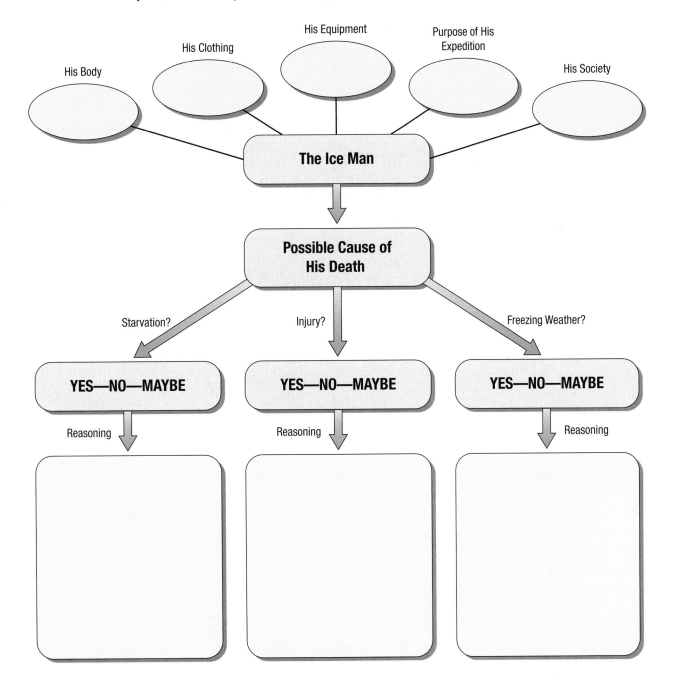

His Body

His Clothing

His Equipment

Purpose of His Expedition

His Society

The Ice Man

Possible Cause of His Death

Starvation?

Injury?

Freezing Weather?

YES—NO—MAYBE

YES—NO—MAYBE

YES—NO—MAYBE

Reasoning

Reasoning

Reasoning

Information Organization
Quiz and Summary

Read each question carefully. Use your notes to answer the questions. Do not refer back to the text. When you are finished, write a summary of the article.

1   **a.**   What was the Ice Man wearing when he was found?

_____

      b.   What marks did the Ice Man have on his body?

_____

_____

2   **a.**   What did the Ice Man have with him?

_____

_____

      b.   What might he have been doing before he died?

_____

_____

3   Describe the society that the Ice Man lived in.

_____

_____

4   What are some clues as to how the Ice Man died?

_____

_____

Summary

_____

_____

_____

_____

Dictionary Skills

Read the dictionary entry for each word. Then look at how the word is used in the sentence. Write the number of the correct definition and the synonym or meaning in the space provided. Remember that you may need to change the wording of the definition in order to have a grammatically correct sentence.

1 | **remnant** *n* **1 a** : a usually small part, member, or trace remaining **b** : a small surviving group—often used in *pl* **2** : an unsold or unused end of piece goods

The Ice Man's body still wore (   ) _____ of leather

garments and boots that had been stuffed with straw for insulation.

2 | **ordinary** *adj* **1** : of a kind to be expected in the normal order of events : routine, usual **2** : having or constituting immediate or original jurisdiction; *also* : belonging to such jurisdiction **3 a** : of common quality, rank, or ability **b** : deficient in quality : poor, inferior

The Ice Man had some kind of accident in the course of a perfectly

(   ) _____ trip.

3 | **stable** *adj* **1 a** : firmly established : fixed, steadfast **b** : not changing or fluctuating : unvarying **c** : permanent, enduring **2 a** : steady in purpose : firm in resolution **b** : not subject to insecurity or emotional illness : sane, rational **3 a** *(1)* : placed so as to resist forces tending to cause motion or change of motion *(2)* : designed so as to develop forces that restore the original condition when disturbed from a condition of equilibrium or steady motion **b** *(1)* : not readily altering in chemical makeup or physical state *(2)* : not spontaneously radioactive

The Ice Man and his countrymen lived in a society built around

small, (   ) _____ villages.

By permission. From *Merriam-Webster's Collegiate® Dictionary*, 11th Edition © 2010 by Merriam-Webster, Incorporated (www.Merriam-Webster.com).

4 | **element** *n* **1** **a** : any of the four substances air, water, fire, and earth formerly believed to compose the physical universe **b** *pl* : weather conditions; *esp* : violent or severe weather **c** : the state or sphere natural or suited to a person or thing **2** : a constituent part: as **a** *pl* : the simplest principles of a subject of study : rudiments **b** *(1)* : a part of a geometric magnitude *(2)* : a generator of a geometric figure; *also* : a line or line segment contained in the surface of a cone or cylinder *(3)* : a basic member of a mathematical or logical class or set *(4)* : one of the individual entries in a mathematical matrix or determinant **c** : a distinct group within a larger group or community **d** *(1)* : one of the necessary data or values on which calculations or conclusions are based *(2)* : one of the factors determining the outcome of a process **e** : any of the fundamental substances that consist of atoms of only one kind and that singly or in combination constitute all matter **f** : a distinct part of a composite device **g** : a subdivision of a military unit

The trench provided the Ice Man with shelter from the

( ) _____, and he also had a braided

mat of grass to keep him warm.

F   Word Forms

PART 1

In English, many verbs become nouns by adding the suffix *-ion* or *-tion*, for example, *stimulate (v.), stimulation (n.)*.
 Complete each sentence with the correct form of the words on the left. **Use the correct tense of the verbs, in either the affirmative or the negative form. Use the singular or plural form of the nouns.**

insulate *(v.)*

insulation *(n.)*

1 Nicholas put fiberglass between the outside and inside

walls of his house to provide good _____ . He

also _____ the roof; consequently, he saved

money on his heating bills last winter.

demonstrate *(v.)*

demonstration *(n.)*

② Many power companies provide clear and simple

_____ to their customers on how to save

on utility bills. The companies _____

how to insulate a home and save electricity.

explore *(v.)*

exploration *(n.)*

③ On vacation, we _____ the Adirondack

Mountains. Our _____ will also include

underground caverns.

preserve *(v.)*

preservation *(n.)*

④ Many people are interested in the permanent

_____ of undeveloped land in Alaska.

If we _____ this land now, it will be

exploited by major oil companies.

examine *(v.)*

examination *(n.)*

⑤ When Brian was ill, the doctor carefully

_____ him. Although the

_____ took a long time, Brian finally

learned the cause of his illness.

PART 2

In English, the noun and verb forms of some words are the same, for example,
promise (v.), promise (n.).

    Complete each sentence with the correct form of the words on the left.
**Use the correct tense of the verbs, in either the affirmative or the negative
form. Use the singular or plural form of the nouns. In addition, indicate
whether you are using the verb or the noun form by circling *(v.)* or *(n.).***

alert

① The police department put the town on

_____ after a criminal escaped from
    (v., n.)

the nearby prison. After they _____
                                          (v., n.)

everyone, they began a systematic search of the area

in order to find the escaped convict.

release

2 Film companies in the United States usually

_____ about 20 major films a year. They
(v., n.)

always advertise their new _____ on
(v., n.)

television and radio, and in magazines.

damage

3 The flood caused considerable property

_____ to homes near the river. The muddy
(v., n.)

water ruined many people's homes, but, fortunately,

it _____ any major buildings or
(v., n.)

contaminate the water supply.

repair

4 I called in a plumber to fix the leak under my kitchen

sink. However, he _____ the leak
(v., n.)

properly, and water continued to drip. I decided

to buy a book on plumbing and I made the

_____ myself.
(v., n.)

return

5 Perry is going to the store now, but he

_____ by six o'clock. He is going to take
(v., n.)

back a shirt that doesn't fit. The store accepts both

_____ and exchanges.
(v., n.)

Word Partnership	Use *repair* with:
n.	repair **a chimney**, repair **damage**, repair **equipment**, repair **a roof** **auto** repair, **car** repair, **home** repair, repair **parts**, **road** repair, repair **service**, repair **shop**

Word Partnership	Use *return* with:
v.	**decide to** return, **plan to** return
n.	return **trip** return **a (phone) call** return **to work**

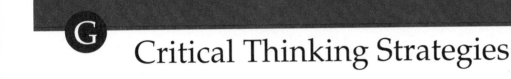

Critical Thinking Strategies

Read each question carefully, and write a response. Remember that there is no one correct answer. Your response depends on what **you** think.

1 In the first paragraph of the article, the author gives a personalized description of what happened to the Ice Man 4,000 years ago and how his friends and family may have felt about his loss. What do you think the tone or feeling of this paragraph is? How is the tone and style different from the rest of the article? Why do you think the author started the article in this way?

_____

_____

_____

_____

2 In the third paragraph, James Shreeve writes that the discovery of the Ice Man "was quite rightly called one of the most important archeological finds of the century." What do you think Shreeve's opinion of this discovery is? Why do you think so?

_____

_____

_____

_____

3 In describing the equipment that the Ice Man had with him, Ian Kinnes points out that they "are not artifacts placed in a grave, but the fellow's own possessions." Why do you think this is so important? Why might objects in a grave be different from what a man normally carries with him for a day or a week?

_____

_____

_____

_____

4 In lines 26–31, the author describes the society that the Ice Man lived in and compares it with the civilizations of the Egyptians and Mesopotamians of the same time period. How do you think James Shreeve knows what the Ice Man's society was like? How does he know what Egyptian and Mesopotamian society was like at that time?

_____

_____

_____

_____

5. The article informs us that "the Ice Man's return from the Tyrol has demonstrated that the local climate is warmer now than it has been for 4,000 years." What inferences can we make from this statement? What do you think may happen in the future as a result of a warmer climate?

_____

_____

_____

H Topics for Discussion and Writing

1. According to Robert Sokal, an evolutionary biologist at the State University of New York at Stony Brook, we need to find many examples of preserved people from 4,000 years ago in order to "make statements about the population that existed at the time." What information do you think we can learn from such discoveries? How might this information be useful to us in the twenty-first century?

2. If you could ask the Ice Man questions about himself and his time, what would you ask? Work with a partner and make a list of questions. Compare your list with your classmates' lists.

3. **Write in your journal.** Imagine that you were the Ice Man 4,000 years ago. Describe your last week alive. Write about what you did, where you went, the people you met, and your last hours.

I Follow-Up Activities

1. Work with a partner or in a small group. Read the passage that follows. This is up-to-date information about the Ice Man. Compare this new information with the original information from the article "Messenger from the Past." If the original information is correct, leave it. If the information is now incorrect, change it. If there is additional information, add it to the chart.

Otzi's Last Days: Glacier Man May Have Been Attacked Twice

ScienceDaily (Feb. 4, 2009)

1   Another chapter in a murder case over 5,000 years old. New investigations by an LMU (Ludwig-Maximilians-Universitat Munich) research team working together with a Bolzano colleague reconstructed the chronology of the injuries that Ötzi, the glacier man preserved as a frozen mummy, received in his last

5   days. It turns out, for example, that he did in fact only survive the arrow wound in his back for a very short time—a few minutes to a number of hours, but no more—and also definitely received a blow to the back with a blunt object only shortly before his death. In contrast, the cut wound on his hand is some days older. Reports Professor Andreas Nerlich, who led the study, "It is now clear that

10   Ötzi endured at least two injuring events in his last days, which may imply two separate attacks. Although the ice mummy has already been studied at great length, there are still new results to be gleaned. The crime surrounding Ötzi is as thrilling as ever!" It is the oldest ice mummy ever found. Ötzi, the man from the Neolithic Age, is giving science critical information about life more than

15   5000 years ago, not least from his equipment. His copper axe, for example, reveals that metalworking was already much more advanced in that era than was previously assumed. Yet Ötzi's body, too, gives us many details as to his diet, state of health—and not least to his murder.

Some time ago, we detected a deep cut wound on Ötzi's hand that he must

20   have survived for at least a couple of days," says Nerlich, head of the Institute of Pathology at Municipal Hospital Munich-Bogenhausen and member of the Medical Faculty of LMU, Munich. "Another team at about the same time found an arrow tip in Ötzi's left armpit. The shaft of the arrow was missing, but there is an entry wound on the back." It is probable, in that case, that the man died

25   of internal bleeding because the arrow hit a main artery. What was unclear, however, was the age and exact chronology of the injuries.

Now, Nerlich has reconstructed the missing chronology while working together with LMU Munich forensic scientist Dr. Oliver Peschel and Dr. Eduard Egarter-Vigl, head of the Institute for Pathology in Bolzano. According to the

30   new information, Ötzi did in fact only survive the arrow wound for a very short period of time, of no more than a few hours. "Ötzi had only shortly survived the arrow wound and the blow on the back," Nerlich summarizes. "At least a couple of days before his death, however, he sustained a severe cut wound on his right hand. Over several days, then, Ötzi suffered at least two injuring events—which

35   could point towards two separate attacks."

	Original Information (Source): "Messenger from the Past"—Discover	Revised Information (Source): "Otzi's Last Days: Glacier Man May Have Been Attacked Twice"
When the Ice Man lived	4,000 years ago	
The Age the Ice Man lived in	the Bronze Age	
The Cause of the Ice Man's Death	(unknown)	
The Ice Man's physical condition	uninjured	
The marks on the Ice Man's body	tattoos on his back and behind his knee	
The Ice Man's equipment	clothes made of leather a bronze ax a bow, arrows, and a quiver	
Other Information		

2 According to this article, the Ice Man lived 4,000 years ago in the Bronze Age. His society was very different from the civilizations of Egypt and Mesopotamia of the same time period. Select an area of the world, perhaps your own. Refer to the chart below. In pairs or small groups, select one of the Ages and find out what characterizes each Age. Then refer to the Internet, a history book or an encyclopedia, or your own knowledge. What Age best describes the society you chose? Write a description of what life was like 5,000 years ago for the people in the society you have chosen. Discuss how their lives and the lives of Ice Man and his people were similar and how they were different.

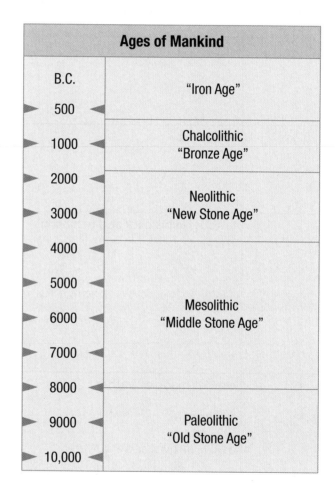

Ages of Mankind	
B.C.	"Iron Age"
▶ 500 ◀	
▶ 1000 ◀	Chalcolithic "Bronze Age"
▶ 2000 ◀	
▶ 3000 ◀	Neolithic "New Stone Age"
▶ 4000 ◀	
▶ 5000 ◀	
▶ 6000 ◀	Mesolithic "Middle Stone Age"
▶ 7000 ◀	
▶ 8000 ◀	
▶ 9000 ◀	Paleolithic "Old Stone Age"
▶ 10,000 ◀	

Cloze Quiz

Complete the passage with words from the list. Use each word only once.

ancestral	contained	exploration	remainder
authority	culture	furthermore	revealed
circumstances	details	hunting	society
civilizations	die	illness	starve
clearly	evidence	probably	unlike

_____ the Egyptians and Mesopotamians of the
(1)

time, who had more advanced _____ with cities and
(2)

central _____ , the Ice Man and his countrymen lived in
(3)

a _____ built around small, stable villages. He
(4)

_____ spoke in a tongue _____ to current
(5)   (6)

European languages. _____ , though he was a member of a
(7)

farming _____ , he may well have been _____
(8)   (9)

when he died, to add meat to his family's diet. X-rays of the quiver showed

that it _____ 14 arrows. While his backpack was empty,
(10)

careful _____ of the trench where he died _____
(11)   (12)

remnants of animal skin and bones at the same spot where the pack lay.

There was also the _____ of a pile of berries.
(13)

_____ the man didn't _____ to death.
(14)   (15)

So why did the Ice Man _____ ? If injury or
(16)

_____ caused the Ice Man's death, an autopsy on the
(17)

4,000-year-old victim could turn up some clues. The _____
(18)

of his death may have preserved such _____ , as well
(19)

as other _____ of his life.
(20)

Prereading Preparation

1. What is **time travel?** Do you think it is possible? Why or why not?

2. Do you think scientists should try to find a way to travel to the past? To the future? Why, or why not?

3. Would you like to travel to the past? If yes, what year would you like to visit?

4. Would you like to travel to the future? If yes, what year would you like to visit?

5. Using the chart on page 219 as a model, take a survey of your classmates. Compare your classmates' responses.

TIME TRAVEL PREFERENCES				
Student's Name	Would you like to travel to the past? Yes / No	Where would you like to go in the past?	Would you like to travel to the future? Yes / No	Where would you like to go in the future?

Is Time Travel Possible?

1   Contrary to the old warning that time waits for no one, time slows down when you are on the move. It also slows down more as you move faster, which means astronauts someday may survive so long in space that they would return to an Earth of the distant future. If you could move at the speed of light, 186,282

5   miles a second, your time would stand still. If you could move faster than light, your time would move backward.

    Although no form of matter yet discovered moves as fast or faster than light, scientific experiments have confirmed that accelerated motion causes a voyager's, or traveler's, time to be stretched. Albert Einstein predicted this

10 in 1905, when he introduced the concept of relative time as part of his Special Theory of Relativity. A search is now under way to confirm the suspected existence of particles of matter that move faster than light and therefore possibly might serve as our passports to the past.

    An obsession with time—saving, gaining, wasting, losing, and mastering

15 it—seems to have been part of humanity for as long as humans have existed. Humanity also has been obsessed with trying to capture the *meaning* of time. Einstein used a definition of time, for experimental purposes, as that which is measured by a clock. Thus, time and time's relativity are measurable by any

sundial, hourglass, metronome, alarm clock, or an atomic clock that can measure
a billionth of a second.

Scientists have demonstrated that an ordinary airplane flight is like a brief
visit to the Fountain of Youth. In 1972, for example, scientists who took four
atomic clocks on an airplane trip around the world discovered that the moving
clocks moved slightly slower than atomic clocks which had remained on the
ground. If you fly around the world, preferably going eastward to gain the
advantage of the added motion of the Earth's rotation, the atomic clocks
show that you'll return younger than you would have been if you had stayed
home. Frankly, you'll be younger by only 40 billionths of a second. Even
such an infinitesimal saving of time proves that time can be stretched.
Moreover, atomic clocks have demonstrated that the stretching of time
increases with speed.

Here is an example of what you can expect if tomorrow's space-flight
technology enables you to move at ultrahigh speeds. Imagine you're an astronaut
with a twin who stays home.[1] If you travel back and forth to the nearest star
at about half the speed of light, you'll be gone for 18 Earth years. When you
return, your twin will be 18 years older, but you'll have aged only 16 years.
Your body will be two years younger than your twin's because time aboard
the flying spaceship will have moved more slowly than time on Earth. You will
have aged normally, but you have been in a slower time zone. If your spaceship
moves at about 90% of lightspeed, you'll age only 50% as much as your twin.
If you whiz along at 99.86% of lightspeed, you'll age only five percent as much.
These examples of time-stretching, of course, cannot be tested with any existing
spacecraft. They are based on mathematical projections of relativity science.

Speed is not the only factor that slows time; so does gravity. Einstein
determined in his General Theory of Relativity that the force of an object's
gravity "curves" the space in the object's gravitational field. When gravity
curves space, Einstein reasoned, gravity also must curve time, because space
and time are linked.

Numerous atomic clock experiments have confirmed Einstein's calculation
that the closer you are to the Earth's center of gravity, which is the Earth's core,
the slower you will age. In one of these experiments, an atomic clock was taken
from the National Bureau of Standards in Washington, D.C., near sea level, and
moved to mile-high Denver. The results demonstrated that people in Denver age
more rapidly by a tiny amount than people in Washington.

---

[1]This hypothetical situation is known as the Twin Paradox.

If you would like gravity's space-time warp to extend your life, get a home at the beach and a job as a deep-sea diver. Avoid living in the mountains or working in a skyscraper. That advice, like the advice about flying around the world, will enable you to slow your aging by only a few billionths of a second. Nevertheless, those tiny fractions of a second add up to more proof that time-stretching is a reality.

Time Reversal

According to scientific skeptics, time reversal—travel to the past—for humans would mean an unthinkable reversal of cause and effect. This reversal would permit you to do something in the past that changes the present. The skeptics worry that you even might commit an act that prevents your own birth.

Some scientists believe we should keep an open mind about time reversal. Open-minders speculate that time-travelers who change the past would be opening doors to alternative histories, rather than interfering with history as we know it. For example, if you prevented the assassination of Abraham Lincoln, then a new line of historical development would be created. The alternative history—the one without Lincoln's assassination—would have a completely separate, ongoing existence. Thus, no change would be made in anybody's existing history. Another possibility is that nature might have an unbreakable law preventing time travelers from changing the past.

Journey to the Future

If we did discover a source of energy that would enable us to travel beyond lightspeed, we might have access not only to the past, but also to the future. Suppose you went on a super-lightspeed trek to the Spiral Nebula in the Andromeda Galaxy. That location is separated from Earth by 1,500,000 lightyears, the distance light travels in 1,500,000 years. Suppose you make the round trip in just a few moments. If all goes well, you'll return to the Earth 3,000,000 years into its future, because that's how much Earth time will have elapsed.

Time is an abstraction. In other words, it cannot be seen, touched, smelled, or tasted. It seems to have no existence apart from the events it measures, but something tells us that time is out there, somewhere. "When we pursue the meaning of time," according to the time-obsessed English novelist-playwright J. B. Priestly, "we are like a knight on a quest, condemned to wander through innumerable forests, bewildered and baffled, because the magic beast he is looking for is the horse he is riding."

What about our quest for particles that travel faster than light? If we find them, will we be able to control their energy to tour the past? If we return to our past, will we be forced to repeat our mistakes and suffer the same consequences? Or will we be able to use our experience to make everything turn out better the second time around?

Will we ever be able to take instant trips to the distant future, the way people do in the movies, with a twist of a dial and a "Zap!, Zap!" of sound effects? One cannot resist the temptation to respond that only time will tell.

Fact-Finding Exercise

Read the passage again. Then read the following statements. Scan the article quickly to see if they are True (T) or False (F). If a statement is false, rewrite it so that it is true.

1 _____ T _____ F   If you could move at the speed of light, your time would move backward.

_____

2 _____ T _____ F   Scientists have discovered a form of matter that moves as fast as light.

_____

3 _____ T _____ F   Scientists have done experiments which show that the stretching of time increases with speed.

_____

4 _____ T _____ F   Both speed and gravity slow time.

_____

5 _____ T _____ F   The closer you are to the Earth's core, the faster you will age.

_____

6 _____ T _____ F   Some people worry that if you could go back in time, you might change the present.

_____

Reading Analysis

Read each question carefully. Circle the number or letter of the correct answer, or write your answer in the space provided.

1 Read lines 4–5.

   a. What is the speed of light?

     _____

   b. What does **your time would stand still** mean?

     1. Your time would speed up.
     2. Your time would reverse.
     3. Your time would stop.

2 Read lines 9–11: "Einstein predicted **this** in 1905." What does **this** refer to? In other words, what did Einstein predict?

   _____

   _____

3 Read lines 11–13.

   a. **Under way** means that the search is

     1. being done now
     2. finished
     3. under a method

   b. **Suspected existence** means that

     1. people have found these particles
     2. people believe these particles exist
     3. people do not believe these particles exist

   c. What are our **passports to the past?**

   _____

   _____

4 Read lines 21–22. In this sentence, scientists mean that an airplane trip might

    a. make you younger
    b. speed up the aging process
    c. make you older

5 Read line 28. **Frankly** means

    a. actually
    b. on the contrary
    c. obviously

6 In lines 28–29, an **infinitesimal** saving of time is

    a. a large amount
    b. an average amount
    c. a very small amount

7 In lines 32–33, **tomorrow** refers to

    a. the day after today
    b. some time in the future
    c. some time next year

8 Read lines 33–38.

    a. What is this imaginary situation commonly known as?

    _____

    _____

    _____

    b. How do you know?

    _____

    c. **Back and forth** means

        1. travel to the nearest star and then return to Earth
        2. travel to the nearest star two times
        3. travel back to the nearest star after you've been there

9 Read line 41. **Whiz** means
   a. age
   b. change
   c. move

10 Read lines 44–46. Why is **"curves"** in quotation marks?

_____

_____

11 Read lines 70–74. What is this imaginary situation an example of?

_____

_____

12 Read lines 75–76. What is the purpose of **did?**
   a. To ask a question
   b. To show emphasis
   c. To express the past

13 In lines 79–80, what does **round trip** mean?

_____

_____

14 Read lines 84–88.
   a. What does **quest** mean?

_____

_____

   b. How do you know?

_____

_____

_____

Information Organization

Read the article again. Underline what you think are the main ideas. Then scan the article and complete the following table, using the sentences that you have underlined to help you. You will use this table later to answer specific questions about the article. Not all the boxes will be filled in.

	Speed	Gravity
Time speeds up		
Time slows down		
Time stops		
Experimental evidence		
Hypothetical example		

Information Organization Quiz and Summary

Read each question carefully. Use your notes to answer the questions. Do not refer back to the text. When you are finished, write a brief summary of the article.

1 How does the speed of light affect time?

_____

_____

2 Describe the evidence which shows that time is affected by speed.

_____

_____

3 Describe the evidence which shows that time is affected by gravity.

_____

_____

4 How would time reversal change cause and effect?

_____

_____

Summary

_____

_____

_____

_____

_____

_____

Dictionary Skills

Read the dictionary entry for each word. Then look at how the word is used in the sentence. Write the number of the correct definition and the synonym or meaning in the space provided. Remember that you may need to change the wording of the definition in order to have a grammatically correct sentence.

1

> **matter** *n* **1** **a** : a subject under consideration **b** : a subject of disagreement or litigation **c** *pl* : the events or circumstances of a particular situation **d** : the subject or substance of a discourse or writing **e** : something of an indicated kind or having to do with an indicated field or situation **f** : something to be proved in law **g** : *obsolete* : sensible or serious material as distinguished from nonsense or drollery **h** *(1) obsolete* : reason, cause *(2)* : a source *esp* of feeling or emotion **i** : problem, difficulty **2** **a** : the substance of which a physical object is composed **b** : material substance that occupies space, has mass, and is composed predominantly of atoms **3** **a** : the indeterminate subject of reality; *especially* : the element in the universe that undergoes formation and alteration **b** : the formless substratum of all things which exists only potentially and upon which form acts to produce realities . . .

No form of (   ) _____ has yet been discovered that

moves as fast or faster than light.

2

> **stretch** *v* **1** : to extend (as one's limbs or body) in a reclining position **2** : to reach out : extend **3** : to extend in length . . . **6** : to draw up (one's body) from a cramped, stooping, or relaxed position **7** : to pull taut **8** **a** : to enlarge or distend *esp* by force **b** : to extend or expand as if by physical force **c** : strain **9** : to cause to reach or continue (as from one point to another or across a space) **10** **a** : to amplify or enlarge beyond natural or proper limits **b** : to expand (as by improvisation) to fulfill a larger function . . .

Experiments with atomic clocks show that it is possible to

(   ) _____ time.

By permission. From *Merriam-Webster's Collegiate® Dictionary*, 11th Edition © 2010 by Merriam-Webster, Incorporated (www.Merriam-Webster.com).

CHAPTER 12   IS TIME TRAVEL POSSIBLE?

3 **determine** *v* **1** **a** : to fix conclusively or authoritatively **b** : to decide by judicial sentence **c** : to settle or decide by choice of alternatives or possibilities **d** : resolve **2** **a** : to fix the form, position, or character of beforehand : ordain **b** : to bring about as a result : regulate **3** **a** : to fix the boundaries of **b** : to limit in extent or scope **c** : to put or set an end to : terminate **4** : to find out or come to a decision about by investigation, reasoning, or calculation **5** : to bring about the determination of

Einstein (   ) _____ in his General Theory

of Relativity that the force of an object's gravity "curves" the space in

the object's gravitational field.

4 **speculate** *vi* **1** **a** : to meditate on or ponder a subject : reflect **b** : to review something idly or casually and often inconclusively **2** : to assume a business risk in hope of gain; *especially* : to buy or sell in expectation of profiting from market fluctuations *vt* **1** : to take to be true on the basis of insufficient evidence: theorize **2** : to be curious or doubtful about: wonder <speculates whether it will rain all vacation>

Open-minders (   ) _____ that time-travelers

who change the past would be opening doors to alternative histories,

rather than interfering with known history.

By permission. From *Merriam-Webster's Collegiate® Dictionary*, 11th Edition © 2010 by Merriam-Webster, Incorporated (www.Merriam-Webster.com).

UNIT 4   SCIENCE AND TECHNOLOGY

F   Word Forms

In English, some verbs become nouns by adding the suffix *-ance* or *-ence*, for example, *appear (v.)*, *appearance (n.)*.

Complete each sentence with the correct form of the words on the left. **Use the correct tense of the verbs, in either the affirmative or the negative form.**

avoid *(v.)*

avoidance *(n.)*

1 Monica regularly _____ exposure to the sun. Her careful _____ of the sun is due to persistent skin problems.

resist *(v.)*

resistance *(n.)*

2 It is a well-known fact that stress lowers the body's _____ to illness. It is logical, then, that we _____ disease better when we maintain good health and avoid stressful situations.

accept *(v.)*

acceptance *(n.)*

3 Gloria's English teacher _____ any papers that are more than two days late. This is her policy. Her professor's _____ of papers also depends on whether the students have followed her guidelines for the format of the paper, such as double spacing.

insist *(v.)*

insistence *(n.)*

4 Arthur invariably _____ on having dinner at the same time every day. His _____ on the same dinnertime isn't his only odd habit. He also insists on eating the same breakfast, and going to the same place for vacation every year.

exist (v)

existence (n.)

5 There is a myth about a creature called the Abominable Snowman, which some people believe _____ somewhere in the Himalaya Mountains. There is also a legend about the _____ of a giant creature called Sasquatch, or Bigfoot, which supposedly lives in the Pacific Northwest.

PART 2

In English, some verbs become adjectives by adding the suffix -al, for example, cause (v.), causal (adj.).

Complete each sentence with the correct form of the words on the left. **Use the correct tense of the verbs, in either the affirmative or the negative form.**

survive (v.)

survival (adj.)

1 Mark and Laura were stranded in the mountains in the middle of a severe snowstorm. They needed basic _____ skills in order to stay alive. They _____ the bitter cold because they found a small cave, which protected them from the harsh weather until a rescue team found them two days later.

arrive (v.)

arrival (n.)

2 Ted's children eagerly awaited the _____ of their father at the airport. When Ted finally _____ , the children greeted him very excitedly. He had been away for a long time!

experiment *(v.)*

experimental *(adj.)*

3 Scientists in the pharmaceutical laboratory are working on a new drug, but it is in the _____ stage. Doctors cannot prescribe it yet. The scientists _____ successfully with the drug in the laboratory; now they need to test it on human volunteers.

cause *(v.)*

causal *(adj.)*

4 When researchers try to establish what _____ a given disease, they look for relationships between certain factors and the onset of the disease. Sometimes it is difficult to establish a clear _____ relationship between the disease and a particular factor.

Word Partnership	Use *experiment* with:
v.	**conduct an** experiment, **perform an** experiment, **try an** experiment
adj.	**scientific** experiment, **simple** experiment

Word Partnership	Use *cause* with:
v.	**determine the** cause, **support a** cause
n.	cause **of death,** cause **an accident,** cause **cancer,** cause **problems,** cause **a reaction,** cause **for concern**

Critical Thinking Strategies

Read each question carefully, and write a response. Remember that there is no one correct answer. Your response depends on what **you** think.

1 In line 1 of the article, the author refers to a proverb, "Time waits for no one." What do you think this proverb means? Why do you think the author mentioned this proverb with regard to the topic of the reading?

_____

_____

_____

2 Read lines 42–44. Why do you think time-stretching cannot be tested with any spacecraft we have today?

_____

_____

_____

3 Read lines 61–65. What do you think **reversal of cause and effect** means? What do you think about this argument against travel to the past?

_____

_____

_____

4 Read lines 82–88. What do you think is the purpose of this reference to a knight on a quest? In other words, what image do you think the author wants us to visualize? Why?

_____

_____

_____

UNIT 4   SCIENCE AND TECHNOLOGY

Topics for Discussion and Writing

1. Imagine that you could travel to the past. What is the one historical event you would like to change? Why do you want to change it? How would you change it? What consequences might this change have for the present?

2. Would you like to see the future? Why? What year do you want to visit? Explain.

3. Imagine that time travel is possible. Do you think there should be restrictions on this type of travel? For example, many countries have visa and immigration restrictions. Should there also be restrictions on time travel? If so, what restrictions do you suggest? Who would be in charge of making these rules and enforcing them?

4. **Write in your journal.** Imagine that you could travel back in time. Choose a person from the past you would like to meet. Explain why you would like to meet this person.

Follow-Up Activities

1. a. Refer to the Time Preference Survey on page 236. Discuss it in class to make sure you understand the questions.
   b. With a partner or alone, go outside your class and survey two or three people.
   c. Bring back your data and combine it with the other students' information. Create a bar graph or other chart to compile your data. Divide your responses by past, present, and future. Then divide those responses by gender and/or by age. What do you observe about the responses? Are there any observable patterns by gender or by age? Speculate on the reasons why these groups prefer a particular time.

TIME PREFERENCE SURVEY			
	1	2	3
Informant's Gender (M / F)			
Informant's Age Group (under 20 / 20–25 / 26–30 / 31–35 / 36–40 / 41+)			
1. If you could travel through time, when would it be: the past / the present / the future?			
2. If you prefer the past, why would you go back?			
3. If you prefer the present, why would you stay here?			
4. If you prefer the future, why would you go there?			

UNIT 4   SCIENCE AND TECHNOLOGY

Cloze Quiz

Complete the passage with words from the list. Use each word only once.

concept	light	return	survive
contrary	motion	slows	than
experiments	move	space	time
faster	part	speed	waits
future	predicted	still	yet

_____ to the old warning that time _____ for
    (1)   (2)

no one, _____ slows down when you are on the move. It also
          (3)

_____ down more as you move _____ ,
    (4)   (5)

which means astronauts someday may _____ so long in
                                           (6)

_____ that they would _____ to an Earth of the
    (7)   (8)

distant _____ . If you could move at the _____ of
          (9)   (10)

light, 186,282 miles a second, your time would stand _____ .
                                                           (11)

If you could move faster _____ light, your time would
                              (12)

_____ backward.
    (13)

    Although no form of matter _____ discovered moves
                                          (14)

as fast or faster than _____ , scientific _____
                            (15)   (16)

have confirmed that accelerated _____ causes a voyager's,
                                       (17)

or traveler's, time to be stretched. Albert Einstein _____ this
                                                            (18)

in 1905, when he introduced the _____ of relative time as
                                       (19)

_____ of his Special Theory of Relativity.
    (20)

Crossword Puzzle

Read the clues on the next page. Write the answers in the correct spaces in the puzzle.

Crossword Puzzle Clues

3. The same
4. The past tense of **put**
5. The Ice Man had an _____ made of copper.
6. A dead body
8. The past tense of **write**
10. Our house has _____ in the walls to help keep it warm in the winter.
13. The two countries want to _____ a peace treaty.
18. The past tense of **come**
19. The police look for clues, or _____ , to help them solve crimes.
20. The universe is made up of _____

1. Harry is on a _____ to find the truth.
2. In addition
5. _____ is the coldest place on Earth.
7. Usual; routine
9. Is it possible to _____ , or extend, time?
11. People often _____ , or wonder, about the possibility of time travel.
12. Many scientists believe in the _____ of life on other planets.
14. We need a lot of gear, or _____ , when we go camping in the woods.
15. Many businesses around the world would like to _____ Antarctica's natural resources.
16. The middle of the desert is a very _____ and lonely place.
17. Area; location

Discussion

1. Modern technology has given us insights into the past, the present, and the future. What do you think is the greatest technological advance we have made so far? How will it help us better understand the past, the present, and the future?

2. If time travel to the past were possible today, it would be very easy for us to learn about ancient civilizations. Imagine that time travel to the future is also possible. What do you think would be the biggest advantage to knowing the future? What would be the biggest disadvantage? Explain your answer.

3. Imagine that you could travel 500 years into the future in Antarctica. What do you think you would see there? What country or countries would "own" Antarctica? Why? Explain your answer.

4. People sometimes want to save a "picture" of the time they live in for people in the future to see. They select objects to preserve so that people can look at them at a specific time in the future. A time capsule is a sealed container that people use in order to preserve these objects. You are a member of a committee whose job it is to prepare a time capsule for this year. The time capsule will not be opened until the year 3000. Discuss with the other members of your committee what you would like to put into the time capsule in order to show what this year was like.

Words in blue are on the Academic Word List (AWL), Coxhead (2000). The AWL is a list of the 570 highest-frequency academic word families that regularly appear in academic texts. The list was compiled by researcher Averil Coxhead from a corpus of 3.5 million words.

A

abstraction 221
accumulation 97
acknowledge 160
acupuncture 75
adolescence 97
advanced 200
advice 3, 221
ailments 76
alternative 221
anatomy 143
ancestral 200
anger 59
annoyance 21
annoying 21
approval 21, 97, 121
archeological 200
arthritis 76
articles 119
artifacts 200
Asian 75, 97, 159
assassination 221
assumption 37
astronauts 219
atomic 220
attributes 183
auditory 143
autopsy 200
avoid 3, 143, 221
ax 200

B

backward 219
baffled 222

balance 76, 120
bans 183
behavioral 21
bewildered 222
bill 121, 160
billionth 220
birth order 37
bond 21
bonding 21
bottom out 98
branches 120
Bronze Age 200
build-up 59

C

came to a head 184
capacity 3
cardiology 59
Caucasian 75, 97
cause and effect 221
celebrity 200
characteristics 22
chats 143
checks and balances 120
cholesterol 59
chore 143
chromosomes 201
circumstances 201
civilizations 200
claim 37, 184
clientele 159
clues 3, 184, 201
coexist 3
cognitive 143

colonial 119
commensurate 161
common sense 3
compete 161
competence 38, 98
competition 161
complex 183
concern 98, 201
concluded 37, 75
conclusion 4, 38, 159
condemned 221
conduct 38
confederation 119
conflict 183
confusion 21
congress 119
considerable 76
contend 183
continent 183
contrary 219
contribute 98
conventional 76
cope 98
coronary 59
corpse 200
crisis 162
cruise 183
cure 76
currents 161, 183
cutbacks 159

D

dedicated 184
demographer 38
depletion 184
depression 76
deprive 183
destiny 38
diagnosis 75
differentiates 21
dilemma 120
diluted 38
discomfort 75

discontent 119
discredited 37
dismissed 184
disproportionate 37
dissection 143
distant 200, 219, 222
domination 119
drafting 121
drop 97, 144, 183
dying breed 21

E

ecological 184
Egyptians 200
electrodes 75
elements 200
elite 159
elitism 160
emerged 201
emphasis 21, 98, 160
endanger 120
endorsement 21
endothelium 59
energetically 76
enforced 121
environment 4, 144
environmentalists 183
erase 120
estimate 75, 144, 183
eternal 121
everyday 4, 59, 200
evidence 37, 98, 144, 201
evolution 119
excruciating 75
executive 76, 120
expedition 200
experimental 219
expertise 161
experts 37, 144, 201
exploitation 183
exploration 183, 200
extend 183, 221
extraordinarily 119

extraordinary 3
extreme 184

F
factors 37
far more 160
fare 98
feminized 22
flexibility 160
food chain 183
foreword 120
foundation 119, 184
Fountain of Youth 220
fragile 201
framework 119
frankly 220
fraternal twins 3
freeze-dried 200
frigid 183, 201
frontier 183
functions 120

G
gain 71, 219
gear 200
generate 183
genetic 3, 201
glacier 200, 214
genuinely 200
global warming 184
grave 200
gravitational 220
gravity 220
guarantee 119
guarded 121

H
handful 184
heart disease 59
heritage 3
hikers 200
hiking 200
honoring 21

hostility 59
hubby 21

I
icebergs 183
identical 3, 144, 160
identity 22
impact 37, 97, 144
implies 3
in all 75, 184
in jeopardy 98
in other words 121, 221
in vain 75
inadequate 120
include 3, 37
inconvenience 21
indications 184
individual 3, 21, 97, 120, 201
individualism 21
individuality 120
infinite 160
inflate 97
inherited 144
inhospitable 183
initial 119
initially 160
innumerable 222
insist 161
instead 60, 76, 97
insulated 200
insulation 200
insure 120
intellectual 144
intelligence 37, 144
interfering 221
involuntarily 75
irresistible 183
isolation 184

J
jeopardize 183, 201
judiciary 120
junior 21, 160
justice 120

K

kinesthetic 143

L

largely 3
laughter 59
launch 97
learning styles 143
legal 119
legislature 120
liberties 120
lifespan 97
liken 97
link 183
locked away 183
lured 183
luxury 160

M

majority 119
malleable 144
manipulating 144
measure 3, 59, 76, 159, 220
medicine 59, 75
melt 183
mere 121, 183
Mesopotamians 200
mineral 183
miserable 3
missions 162
mixed bag 21
motion 71, 219
motivation 38

N

namesake 21
needles 75
negotiated 184
neurologist 75
nevertheless 221
nonexistent 37
noticeable 76
novel 97
nowadays 21, 75

O

obligation 22
obsession 219
obvious 119, 143
offspring 3
omnastics 21
on the one hand 120
on the other hand 3, 38, 120, 161
one-shot 76
ongoing 221
optional 161
options 121, 161
organs 76, 201
orthopedist 75
overall 98, 119
overheating 183

P

paradox 3
participate 4, 71, 97
particles 219
perceive 159
perform 161
phenomena 184
plunge 97
pollute 183
pose 143, 184
possessions 200
potential 160
powerful 97, 120
predict 143, 184, 219
predictable 38
predictor 37
predisposed 97
predisposition 3
preserved 201, 214
preserving 183
prevent 59, 121
preventive 59, 76
pricked 75
pride 120
primarily 184
principles 120
privileged 159

projections 220
psychologist 3, 37
put on ice 201
puzzles out 201

Q
qualify 160
quest 221
quiver 200

R
range 4
recognition 3
recover 201
reflect 161, 183
relationship 3
relative 219
relativity 219
reluctantly 119
remainder 200
remnants 200
remote 183
replace 119
republics 119
reserve 183
reshape 119
resigned 200
resist 222
resources 159, 184
responsive 4, 161
restrict 119, 184
reversal 221
rigor 160
rivalry 37
run in 3

S
scale 97
second-class citizens 143
seekers 183
select 4, 160
self-esteem 38, 97
self-fulfilling prophecy 37
selfish 37

sensation 75
sense of humor 59
separated 4, 144, 221
sessions 71
shelter 200
siblings 37
significant 59
simultaneously 143
sites 184
skeptical 76
skeptics 221
slipped 75
so far 185
soak up 160
sole 119
solely 161
solution 120
solvable 143
source 21, 221
sovereignty 184
space-flight 220
spacing 38
spasms 75
spearhead 97
species 183
specific 76, 119, 160
specimens 201
spectacular 185
speculate 221
stable 200
stimulate 76, 161
stress 59, 76, 97, 121
stretch 71, 219
structure 76, 143
subjective 3
subsequently 160
suffer 59, 222
suggest 3, 38
superficial 98
surgery 59, 76
survey 37, 97
survive 160, 200, 214
suspected 219
system 76, 119, 160

T

talent 3
tattooed 200
technology 71, 220
teem 183
temptation 222
tend to 98, 159
that's that 4
thaw 201
theory 37, 219
threat 184
tools 200
tracts 184
traits 4, 22
transition 97
treasure 183
trek 221
trench 200
twitch 75

U

ultimately 22, 59, 183
underestimated 144
underscored 22

V

vast 183
veto 121
vice versa 3
vigilance 121
vigilant 121
vigorous 144, 161
visual 143
vital 183
voyager 219
vulnerable 98

unique 22, 183
unparalleled 183
unprecedented 200
unrivaled 161
upswing 98

W

wander 221
warp 221
well-adjusted 38
well-being 3, 98
wisdom 37

GRAMMAR AND USAGE

Word forms

Adjectives that become adverbs by adding *-ly*, 85, 152

Adjectives that become nouns by adding *-ity*, 67–68, 170–171

Adjectives that become nouns by deleting final *-t* and adding *-ce*, 47–48, 68–69, 131–132, 171–172

Identical verb and noun forms, 30–31, 106–107, 209–210

Verbs that become adjectives by adding *-able*, 153–154

Verbs that become adjectives by adding *-al*, 232–233

Verbs that become nouns by adding *-ance* or *-ence*, 13–14, 231–232

Verbs that become nouns by adding *-ion* or *-tion*, 12–13, 29, 86–87, 107–108, 193–194, 208–209

Verbs that become nouns by adding *-ment*, 46–47, 132–133, 194–195

Word partnership, 14, 31, 48, 69, 87, 108, 133, 154, 172, 195, 211, 233

LISTENING/SPEAKING

Discussion, 16, 32, 50, 55, 70, 89, 110, 116, 135, 155, 159, 174, 180, 182, 197, 213, 235, 240

Group activities, 36, 90–94, 96, 136, 142, 159, 197, 213, 240

Partner activities, 174, 176, 182, 197, 213, 235–236

Surveys, 51, 72, 118, 159, 176, 218–219, 235–236

READING

Comprehension

Critical thinking strategies, 14–16, 31–32, 49–50, 69–70, 87–88, 109–110, 134–135, 154–155, 173–174, 196, 211–213, 234

Information organization, 8–10, 26–28, 43–44, 64–66, 81–83, 103–104, 127–130, 148–150, 167–168, 190–192, 205–206, 227–228

Main ideas, 8–9, 43, 64, 81, 127, 148, 167, 190, 205, 227

Multiple-choice questions, 6–7, 24–25, 40–42, 62–63, 78–80, 100–102, 123–126, 146–147, 163–166, 187–189, 203–204, 224–226

Scanning for information, 5, 23, 39–40, 61, 64, 77, 99, 122, 127, 145, 148, 162, 167, 185, 202, 223

Short-answer questions, 6–7, 24, 41–42, 62–63, 78–79, 100, 102, 123, 125–126, 164, 166, 187–189, 203–204, 224–226

True/False questions, 5, 23, 39–40, 61, 77, 99–100, 122–123, 145, 162–163, 185–186, 202, 223

Dictionary skills, 11, 28, 45, 66–67, 84, 105, 130–131, 151, 169, 192–193, 207–208, 229–230

Group activities, 90–94, 213

Jigsaw reading, 90–94, 136–140

Prereading preparation, 2, 20, 36, 58–59, 74, 96, 118, 142, 158–159, 182, 199, 218–219

Vocabulary, 11, 28, 45, 66–67, 84, 105, 130–131, 151, 169, 192–193, 207–208, 229–230

TECHNOLOGY

Internet research, 33, 216

TOPICS

Acupuncture, 74–95

Antarctica, 182–198

Birth order, 36–55

College education, 158–180

Federal system of government, 118–141

Happiness, 2–19

Ice Man, 199–217

Laughter, 58–73

Names, 20–35

Self-esteem, 96–116

Teachers and students, 142–157

Time travel, 218–240

WRITING

Charts, 18, 26, 33, 36, 64, 96, 103, 111, 140, 142, 148, 167, 175, 182, 205, 215, 235–236

Cloze quizzes, 19, 34–35, 52, 72–73, 95, 112–114, 141, 157, 177–178, 198, 217, 237

Compositions, 16, 89, 197

Crossword puzzles, 53–54, 114–115, 178–179, 238–239

Descriptions, 216

Fill in blanks, 19, 34–35, 52, 72–73, 95, 105, 106–108, 112–114, 130–133, 141, 151–154, 157, 169, 170–172, 177–178, 192–195, 198, 207–210, 217, 229–233, 237

Group activities, 2, 33, 36, 51, 72, 89, 135, 140, 142, 159, 175–176, 180, 197

Guidelines, 180, 197

Journal/diary entries, 16, 32, 50, 70, 89, 110, 135, 155, 174, 197, 213, 235

Letters, 174

Lists, 16–17, 36, 89, 156, 159, 174–175, 180, 197, 213

Outlines, 8–9, 43, 81–82, 127–128, 190–191

Partner activities, 16–17, 51, 156, 174, 213

Sentences, 14–16, 27–28, 36, 49–50, 65–66, 109–110, 134–135, 154–155, 173–174, 191–192, 196, 211–213, 228, 234

Short-answer questions, 6–7, 27, 44–48, 52, 64, 66–70, 82–84, 87–88, 94, 104, 109–110, 129, 149–150, 164, 166, 168, 187–189, 203–204, 206, 224–226

Summaries, 10, 28, 44, 66, 83, 104, 130, 150, 168, 192, 206, 228

Surveys, 51, 118, 159, 176, 236

Tables, 227

Topics for, 16, 32, 50, 70, 89, 110, 135, 155, 174, 197, 213, 235